Grace at the Garbage Dump

Grace at the Garbage Dump

Making Sense of Mission in the Twenty-First Century

❧

JESSE A. ZINK

For Bishop Stephen,
on the occasion of
my licensing

Jesse A. Zink
24 oct. 2012

CASCADE *Books* · Eugene, Oregon

GRACE AT THE GARBAGE DUMP
Making Sense of Mission in the Twenty-First Century

Cascade Books
An Imprint of Wipf and Stock Publishers
199 W. 8th Ave., Suite 3
Eugene, OR 97401

www.wipfandstock.com

ISBN 13: 978-1-61097-613-8

Cataloging-in-Publication data:

Zink, Jesse A.

   Grace at the garbage dump : making sense of mission in the twenty-first
century / Jesse A. Zink

   y + 174 p. ; 23 cm. —Includes bibliographical references.

   ISBN 13: 978-1-61097-613-8

   1. Missions, America — Africa. 2. Missions — South Africa. I. Title

BV3500 .G82 2012

Manufactured in the U.S.A.

*To my parents
for their unfailing support*

Missionaries have on the whole been a feeble folk, not very wise, not very holy, not very patient. They have broken most of the commandments and fallen into every conceivable mistake. And yet God has used their weakness to bring into existence a universal church . . . And there is no reason whatever to suppose that God is incapable of doing to-day what He has done in the past.

—Stephen Neill, *The Unfinished Task* (1957)

Contents

One

"You Have Ruined Your Life"

THE MEN CAME RUSHING into the clinic one Friday morning out of breath. "Come quickly," they said. "Fumanekile is very sick."

Jenny and I looked at each other. Fumanekile was one of our patients who had both tuberculosis and AIDS. He came to the clinic every day to take his TB pills. I had been driving him to appointments for the last several weeks so he could begin antiretroviral treatment for the AIDS. We knew he was ill but his condition must have worsened overnight.

Following the men, we found Fumanekile in his shack, a tiny, cramped, and run-down looking place that wasn't more than seven feet square. An old set of springs with a grungy mattress on top barely fit against one wall. On the other side was a small cooking area. I could see daylight through the pieces of tin and old car parts that served as walls. The tarp that doubled as both ceiling and roof was so low I had to bend over to fit inside. It was a clean and well-maintained place but it was still deeply poor, one of many similarly precarious shacks built in this shantytown community called Itipini.

Fumanekile was lying on his bed, unconscious and gasping for breath. His pulse, when I felt for it, was weak and irregular. It was clear he had to go to the hospital. I helped arrange him on our stretcher and we carefully carried him back up the hill to the clinic and laid him in the bed of our waiting truck. Jenny needed to stay behind to keep the clinic open but a visiting friend of mine agreed to drive. Fumanekile's friend,

Noxolo, climbed up front as well. That left me to climb in the back with Fumanekile, still unconscious and now incontinent. The canopy over the truck bed wasn't very tall so I had to crawl around his body to position myself close to his head. We began bumping slowly along the rutted dirt road that led away from our clinic and into town.

Before moving to South Africa, I had been an emergency medical technician and was used to riding in the back of an ambulance with patients in distress. On an ambulance, I'd have looked for a portable oxygen canister. But we didn't have those in the truck, which was variously used to transport people, food, construction supplies, and a whole host of other items. I thought about taking Fumanekile's pulse and blood pressure. But the road was so bad, the canopy so low, and the ride so bumpy and stop-and-go I could barely manage to arrange myself properly.

Feeling helpless, I started talking to Fumanekile. It didn't matter that he was unconscious. It didn't even matter that he didn't speak English. His first and only language was Xhosa, the African language spoken widely among our patients. Talking was about all I could do.

I told him how much I appreciated his role in my life these past three months that I had been working in Itipini. I had felt overwhelmed by the cultural, racial, and language differences when I arrived. Immersing myself in caring for the TB patients had proven to be a way to begin to cross those barriers. Every day, when he came for his medication, we had made a connection that revolved around a handshake, a mangled Xhosa greeting on my part, and a head nod on his. I told him how hard it had been to watch him get weaker and weaker as time passed, how I had seen how he needed to take longer and longer breaks on the bench in the clinic before he had the energy to walk home again. I wanted so desperately for him to get better, and each time we went to a doctor's appointment, I found myself fervently hoping he would get the all-important antiretrovirals. At each appointment, however, we were told he needed more work done—a chest x-ray, blood work, another TB test—and that the ARVs couldn't be prescribed on that visit. I told him how each time we were told to come back again for another appointment, I thought to myself, "I hope Fumanekile is still alive then." And now it looked like this was it. He had been pushed too far and his body was finally beginning to shut down.

We hit another big bump and I realized there was something I could do for Fumanekile. Crouching in the back of the truck, I took his head in my lap to prevent it from hitting the truck bed on the next bounce. As his head lay cradled there, I began to pray, offering Fumanekile to God's care. Our human care seemed to have done about as much as it could.

The peace of that moment was shattered as soon as we arrived at the casualty unit at the hospital. It struck me as a scene out of a war movie—patients on beds in the hallways, in wheelchairs, and waiting on benches with nurses everywhere but no one apparently in charge. It was immediately distressing. I despaired of ever finding help.

But I knew Fumanekile needed a bed and I knew he needed to be in the ward where it looked like nurses were seeing patients. But with no one clearly in charge, it was hard to know whom to ask for help. The best response to the chaos, it seemed, was to act confident, in control, and knowledgeable, even though I felt none of the three. As I summoned the courage to barge into the ward, I saw two somber-looking men wheeling a coffin out. Inside, I could hear women ululating in grief. Their combination of wailing, crying, and screaming was a terrifying sound to hear for the first time. "Will that be Fumanekile in a few hours?" I thought immediately, looking at the coffin. It was followed closely by a second thought: "There must be a free bed here somewhere!"

There was exactly one free bed but it wasn't going to come easily. I explained Fumanekile's condition as best as I could to the nearest nurse, using the words I remembered from my ambulance department days that sounded most sophisticated and indicative of the worst possible condition. It worked. Noxolo and my friend wheeled Fumanekile in—jumping two other people who were obviously waiting in line on beds outside the door—and the nurses began to examine him. It was a relief to see them put a blood pressure cuff on him and begin to take his vital signs.

I had only ever met Noxolo in passing but I knew enough about her to know she was capable, competent, and caring. I knew she would want to wait with Fumanekile. Not knowing how long that would be, I decided she deserved a chair even as I saw other family members of patients standing next to beds. I went into the hallway but could find only one. It was behind an official-looking desk scattered with official-looking papers. But since there was no official-looking person there, I thought the chair could be put to better use and carried it in to Noxolo, pantomiming the secrecy of the operation. We both laughed. We had done what we could. Now all we could do was wait.

During training just a few months earlier, my missionary colleagues and I had been asked during one session to pick a verb or two we hoped would describe our work. Mine were basic, something like "serve and learn" that reflected a basic Christian posture to the world but also conveyed my eagerness to be open to what the experience could teach me. As I sat with Noxolo I remembered two more creative answers: "advocate" and "stand with."

As we watched Fumanekile continue to struggle for breath, it occurred to me that I had been standing with him these last few months and particularly on this day. It wasn't much—I still wished we had had a fully stocked ambulance—but it was something. And when we had arrived at the hospital, I had become his advocate and ensured he was seen immediately. That advocacy raised uncomfortable questions—did the nurses see him first because he was the most acute patient or because there was a tall white male insisting they do so? And why should I be his advocate only and no one else's? Didn't the two patients we obviously skipped in line deserve an advocate as well? But on that Friday in mid-November, I didn't let myself dwell on those questions.

Fumanekile survived the weekend, though he never regained consciousness. His mother was able to find the money to make the long trek to town from their rural village and see her son comatose in the hospital. But our efforts had been too late. He died a week after we brought him to the hospital. He was twenty-four.

His was not the first name I entered into the register of deaths in the clinic. But it was the first time I could attach specific memories to that name. The work in Itipini was real now, perhaps more vividly, disconcertingly real than I had bargained for.

~

When I was honest with myself, I admitted to myself that I came to South Africa to "save" Africa. Raised in middle-class, educated, and liberal New England, I had been told all my life I was talented and capable, had a bright future, and could do anything I set my mind to. If that was the case, I thought, why not take these talents to a part of the world that needed them most? Why not use my gifts in service to the least among us and rescue them from their obvious despair? I came to South Africa because I had a modest messiah complex.

But I also came to South Africa to follow a story I had only ever known at a distance. I came to South Africa because I wanted to follow to the source the words and pictures sent to us in North America, the stories that told of dying parents, orphaned children, desperate circumstances, stories about AIDS, disease, and death. I had tried for too long to understand these from far away and had become frustrated at the distance. "Africa" was a vast, undifferentiated term for me, something I knew about only in the abstract. I longed to make it particular, vivid, and real.

I came to South Africa to follow a culture and a way of life I knew only around the edges and wished to enter more deeply. I wanted to learn more about the traditions and ways of being in a culture that had experienced such great trauma and yet seemed to have so much to offer. I had heard the desperate stories but I had also heard about the hope and renewal that percolated through the continent. I wanted to know more of that.

I came to South Africa because I knew my faith asked—demanded!—that I do more and be more than what I knew in my familiar and comfortable middle-class surroundings. I came to South Africa because I wanted to know what it was like to be a Christian in a different culture, to be an American in a different country. I wanted to know what it was like to follow in Abraham's footsteps, to leave behind all that was familiar to me, set out on a journey for an unknown land, and use the blessings God had given me to bless others.

Ultimately, I came to South Africa because I knew my life would be incomplete if I never left the comfort in which I was raised. I knew equally well that my experience in South Africa wouldn't complete my life, but it would be less incomplete than if I had never gone.

My move to South Africa was the culmination of a dream I had first had in college of living and working overseas. Yes, it was true there is need in the United States as great as in Africa—the Bronx is much closer to home—but Africa had captured my imagination and been a focus of my education. But my paths had taken me elsewhere, first to graduate school and then to Nome, Alaska, where I reported for a local radio station and joined the volunteer ambulance department. As my time in Nome drew to a close, I knew I had to look abroad once again. Standing on the edge of one continent, my next step had to be off it. I applied to be a missionary of the Episcopal Church, a member of its

Young Adult Service Corps (YASC). YASC asked young Episcopalians to make a yearlong commitment to working with another missionary or diocese somewhere in the Anglican Communion. I had been raised in the church and made my faith my own while in college. YASC—rather than, say, the Peace Corps—appealed to me because it meant I could openly integrate my faith—a powerful motivator for me—into the work I sought to do.

The decision to join YASC raised an important question. Though I am the grandson and great-grandson of Lutheran missionaries in India, *missionary* remained a difficult and loaded word for me, fraught with the mixed history of Christian mission in the non-European world. Missionaries had played a role in extending colonial and imperial dreams. Some had been messengers of subjugation and not liberation who had more effectively preached a kingdom on earth than the kingdom of heaven.

By chance, I was reading Barbara Kingsolver's novel *The Poisonwood Bible* as I filled out the YASC application. As I thought about becoming a missionary, I couldn't help thinking of the righteous and unyielding missionary in the Congo at the center of that story. He refuses to learn about local customs or language, forcibly baptizes people, and preaches a message of sin and hell that emphasized law over grace and was, politely, out of step with the values that motivated my commitment to Christianity. I was interested in working towards the kingdom of God on earth and responding to the real and present physical needs of God's children around the world. Kingsolver's character embodied everything I found wrong with the missionary enterprise. In no way did I want to be associated with him, however fictional he may have been.

But this wasn't the only way to think about mission. Jesus himself had sent his apostles and followers out to preach, proclaim the good news, and, famously, "make disciples of all nations." I couldn't escape this Gospel imperative. Episcopal mission theology stressed the overarching mission of God to draw all creation into right relationship with one another and with God. It was our job to discern our role in this reconciling task. Plus, I learned, the historical picture of mission is complex. It is by no means clear that all missionaries or even most missionaries were as culturally insensitive or imperialistic as I was making them out to be. Indeed, some missionaries had been critical of the gross injustices of the colonial regime virtually from the moment they set foot overseas.

Somehow, I wanted to hold onto the idea of mission and make it my own in the process.

At the same time that I was making peace with the word *mission-ary*, I was also actively fundraising my personal support. YASC paid about half the cost of sending me overseas but that still left ten thousand dollars for me to raise. Raising a sum greater than my net worth was an intimidating prospect. I wrote letter after letter to friends who had been a part of my life. Slowly at first, but growing quickly, money began to pile up. So many people, I realized, were searching in their own way to respond to the stories they heard about life in Africa and other poorer parts of the world. When I approached people who had known me most of my life, that personal connection had a way of unlocking generosity that a donation to a gigantic charity does not.

Beyond buying my plane ticket and providing me health insurance, the fundraising had another important impact. It created a community of people committed to my work, all of whom were praying for me. I departed for South Africa knowing that scores of people, drawn from all parts of my life, cared so much they supported me financially. It was knowledge that gave me great comfort.

When the mission office had asked me what sort of placement I would consider, I had listed three criteria—that it be in sub-Saharan Africa, that it involve work with children so I could return to some of what I remembered and loved from years as a summer camp counselor, and that it involve some medical aspect so that I could continue to follow the passion I had unearthed as an EMT. The mission office suggested I con-sider a placement in Mthatha, South Africa, with Jenny McConnachie, one of the longest-serving missionaries on the Church's mission roster. Jenny ran a community center in a shantytown outside Mthatha that included a preschool and a clinic. It fit my criteria and I readily agreed it was the place for me.

I packed my bags, swapping a subarctic wardrobe for a South African one, visited family members and friends, and got on a plane in mid-August. Two days later, I found myself standing in the Johannesburg airport, confused and exhausted from two long red-eye flights and wondering what sort of place Mthatha could be that I had missed my connection to the only flight of the day there. I would be forced to wait in Jo-burg more than twenty-four hours for the next one.

Not content to wait—I rarely am—I took the advice of the only person I knew in South Africa at the time, the porter who was helping me with my luggage. "Here's what you do," he said. "You take a flight to East London and take the bus to Mthatha." East London was a coastal hub city in the Eastern Cape Province—and a far cry, I would learn, from its namesake city on the Thames River where I had spent the previous day waiting out a long layover. In my bleary-eyed state, it sounded as good a plan as any, so I rebooked the flights and got on another plane. When I arrived around noon, I realized the flaw in the plan was that I hadn't known the bus schedule. Yes, there was a bus to Mthatha that day, I learned, but it didn't leave until ten o'clock that night. But the sun was still shining, the temperature was still warm, and the wind was quiet. The bus station was empty except for a young black woman. I arranged my luggage around me in a corner, exhausted and thinking only about getting to Mthatha in one piece.

As the sun went down, I learned something new and worrisome. The bus station would close at five. I was stunned. After all, what good was a bus station but to wait for the bus? The other woman in the station could see my shock. "Don't worry," she said reassuringly and indicated the drive-through fast food place next door. "This place is open all night and it is well-lighted so we won't be robbed." Robbed? That was doubly shocking. That my safety might be at risk hadn't even occurred to me. I immediately began to worry about my year's worth of luggage—camera, guitar, laptop—and feared it wouldn't make it until the bus arrived. I had come to South Africa to escape my American comfort zone but I hadn't expected to be quite this uncomfortable quite so soon.

The young woman's name was Lebo and we began chatting as the station agent closed down for the evening. She was from Johannesburg and had been in the East London area to visit a traditional healer and bring an end to a string of bad luck in her personal life and at work. "This is the lowest point of my life," she told me. She was convinced someone had placed a spell on her and that she needed to be ritually cleansed.

"You have probably never starved, but look at me," she said soon into our conversation. "I am starving, I am freezing, and I can't pay the bills." I may have been new to South Africa but I knew enough to beware of people preying on my good intentions. My exhaustion made me defensive. She said she was starving but she was more than a little over-weight. Still, she seemed genuine and I thought there might be safety in numbers. The neon lights of the fast food restaurant were comforting and familiar, and I was hungry, so I offered to buy her dinner. We moved over to a picnic table at the restaurant, me dragging all my luggage, her with one small shoulder bag.

As the sun set, the wind picked up. It blew strong and cold off the ocean, drowning out the sound of the waves a mere one hundred yards away. I dug around in my luggage, looking for the only jacket I had packed with me not ever thinking I would need it so soon. I guiltily snuggled into it as I watched Lebo shiver in her thin sweatshirt.

I had been reading about South Africa in preparation for my de-parture—mostly the *Lonely Planet* guidebook—but as she talked about her life, the texture of the country came alive in a way written words could not match. She had a degree in cosmetology but said she couldn't find a job because whenever she showed up for an interview and people saw she was black, they told her the position was full. So she worked in a bar seven days a week. Her parents had died in a car crash when she was eighteen. "If I wrote a book of my life, it would be full of sorrow," she said. "But someday I will come out of Egypt. I look at myself—I am smart, I have a degree, I am not ugly—so why can't I drive a car and have a good job?" I eagerly peppered her with questions during the meal but it was the ones I was too uncomfortable to ask that were most interesting. How could she believe in witchcraft and compare herself to the Israelites leaving Egypt? What did she think about the promise of a nonracial democracy when she still couldn't find the kind of job she wanted? I scribbled down her comments when she took her cigarette breaks and marveled at how much I needed to learn about this country that was to be my new home.

As we finished our meal, a gang of white motorcycle riders pulled in. She glanced at them and said, "When whites ruled, you had to run when you saw them." Motorcyclists had often trailed violence in their wake. On this night, they sat under a neon sign, content, it appeared, simply to strut and preen on their motorcycles.

"How come they can stay here without ordering anything?" I asked. We had had to buy our dinner in order to sit at the picnic table.

She looked at me incredulously. "Look at those boys bringing the food. They're all black. Do you think they're going to ask them to leave?"

Then she added, about the motorcycle gang, "They are probably looking at you, saying, 'What is that white man doing with that black woman?'" I looked around. I hadn't realized we were the only interracial pairing. I might have dwelled on this a little longer but it didn't seem to bother Lebo, and I was too wrapped up in her storytelling to care much about this first exposure to the deep racial divisions that still marked South African society.

Eventually, I began to run dry on questions. Our meal was long gone and we still had hours left to wait for the bus. She turned to me, wanting to know where I was from and why I had all this luggage with me. When I said I was moving to South Africa to work at a community center, she was surprised. Couldn't I find a job in America? Indeed I could, I said, and I told her how I had recently given up a job to move here. "You quit your job to come to this country?" she said uncomprehendingly and, looking directly at me, added: "You know what you have done? You have ruined your life."

Two

At the Dump

I MUST HAVE GIVEN directions to Itipini scores of times—to visitors, friends, the odd social worker who didn't know where her own territory was. Head east out of Mthatha, I would tell them, down the hill past the wholesale grocery store on the right and the run-down mall on the left, and past the last stoplight. In between the last two sets of speed bumps in town, the final barrier before the open road to Port St. John's and the Indian Ocean, there's a turnoff to a small dirt road.

The dirt road first crosses a small bridge, ostensibly designed to direct a small stream under the road. But, I would warn, the culvert underneath is so frequently clogged with trash and debris that as often as not the water flows over the road. If you drive too quickly through that water you'll splash the young men who are washing cars there. If you drive too slowly, you might just get stuck in the middle of the bridge.

As you pass two turnoffs to your right—neither of which you should take, I'd add hastily—the road becomes more pitted and shows few signs of any maintenance or care. It drops down slightly and comes alongside the Mthatha River. When the Mthatha River flows into the Indian Ocean several dozen kilometers from here it's blue and clear. Not here. Here, topsoil runoff has turned the river opaque, a muddy brown that conceals all manner of trash hidden within. During the wet summer, I'd warn, the river can overflow its banks, making the dirt road a mud pit that is difficult to pass.

Cars are rare on this road. No minibus taxis come here from town and no one who lives down this road has a vehicle. But the road is full of foot traffic. In the morning, a small flotilla of men, some pushing modified grocery carts, head into town looking to earn a day's wage in tips carrying groceries and moving other loads. Women follow them, perhaps to go shopping or to make money themselves, selling fruit or sweets from a stand or watching bags and parcels while their owners are shopping. There are older men and women as well, some headed to a liquor store to spend a portion of their pension losing themselves in cheap alcohol.

I gave these directions and landmarks to other people once I had become practiced at getting myself to Itipini. But it was all new to me on a warm August morning, a late winter day that offered a hint of the spring that was just around the corner. I was riding in the back of Jenny's *bakkie*, the same small pickup truck I would be riding in with Fumanekile in a few months. The ride was bumpy over all the ruts and rocks. I struggled to maintain my seat and not hit my head on the canopy. I was eager to see what was coming but also eager to emerge in one piece.

Rounding a corner, heading up a slight hill away from the river, I began to catch the first glimpses of the community I had been sent to be a part of. It was a shantytown: shack after shack, shambolic and tumble-down, made out of old pieces of metal, abandoned car parts, tree branches, tar paper, and even old beer cartons. Whatever had been available to provide some protection from the elements had been used to create a community of shacks, randomly scattered on a hill that rose up from the Mthatha River's edge. This was Itipini.

The road stopped climbing and straightened out, running along a ridge a short way above the river. Below, the shacks were crammed close together along the riverbank. Up above us, the hill continued to rise. The shacks up there were more spread out and had small plots of corn and other vegetables between them.

The dirt road suddenly turned to concrete. Looking out the window, I could see that the buildings up ahead had changed as well. They were made mostly from cinder blocks, and the area between them was paved with cement. It was also refreshingly clear of the trash and broken glass that was scattered throughout the rest of the community. I clambered out and set foot for the first time in the middle of the Itipini Community Project.

In the Xhosa language, Itipini means "at the dump" and the name reflects its origins. People began to live in Itipini when it was the municipal dump so they could scavenge in the refuse. Later, the dump was closed but the shantytown persisted and continued to grow. It is a transient community, so population figures are hard to come by, but a very rough estimate is that between two and three thousand people call Itipini home at any one time. None of the shacks has electricity or running water, except perhaps on rainy days when water leaks through the roofs and walls.

Itipini is not unique in South Africa. There are many similar communities all over the country and, indeed, all over the continent. These "informal settlements," as they are known, are in many ways a step below the township areas that were the hallmark of apartheid-era South Africa. Homes in the historical township areas vary in terms of quality, but many are made of concrete blocks and now usually have a water tap close by and a connection to power lines. Some areas of the townships are improving rapidly, undergoing a process that Americans might call gentrification. But informal settlements like Itipini stubbornly persist and have even expanded since the end of apartheid now that the restrictions on movement and living areas have been lifted.

Itipini lies about a mile outside Mthatha, now a midsized regional economic hub. For twenty or more years, however, Mthatha—occasionally spelled Umtata and pronounced more or less as if the *h* is silent in both cases—was the capital city of the Transkei, a nominally independent country during the apartheid era. The white regime argued that there was no black majority in South Africa but a series of ethnic groups, none of which could claim a majority. White South Africans were one such grouping, as were the many other black ethnicities, like the Sotho, the Swana, and the Zulu. The apartheid government carved out an individual "homeland" or "bantustan" for each group. The result of the policy was to preserve the vast bulk of land for whites and relegate black people to unproductive backwaters. The largest of these was the Transkei, one of two homelands for the Xhosa people. In 1976, the Transkei, under the watchful gaze of the apartheid government, declared its independence.

The Transkei was nominally independent for nearly two decades, though no country but South Africa ever recognized this independence.

A United Nations' resolution at the time called it "sham independence" and said it was designed only to perpetuate apartheid policies. Its leaders were puppets of the apartheid regime. The country received almost no infrastructure or educational investment. Businesses that had been operating in the region before independence packed up and left. The region was and is predominantly rural. Independence meant that its citizens were confined to their villages, forced to eke out a living with subsistence agriculture but without the benefit of modern farming equipment or education. Even today, the rural parts of the region are marked by huge tracts of eroded and uncultivated land, the result of poor farming practices that have spanned generations.

The Xhosa people[*] are one of the largest language groupings in South Africa, populating virtually all of the Eastern Cape province and stretching as far south and west as Cape Town. But the Transkei is the heartland of the Xhosa. Many of the revolutionary leaders of the African National Congress came from the region that became the Transkei, men like Nelson Mandela, Oliver Tambo, Chris Hani, and Thabo Mbeki. The Xhosa people speak a language that bears their name. Because English was not taught very rigorously in the Transkei, many people—particularly poorer ones of older generations—speak little to no English and can barely read or write their own language. Some in the younger generations speak at least a little English but it remains a distinctly second, third, or fourth language in the region.

The Transkei no longer exists as a separate country, but the old borders are still visibly evident. Drive the N2 highway from Kokstad to Mthatha and it becomes clear when you have entered the Transkei. The infrastructure is worse, the soil erosion obvious, and the houses more run-down. The communities just seem poorer.

While Mthatha is now fully a part of South Africa, it has a reputation for violence and crime that was best summarized for me by a guesthouse owner I met while traveling in a rich, predominantly white town in another province. When I told him where I lived, all he could think to say in response was, "Who did you have to kill to get sent to Mthatha?" his voice dripping with scorn. During vacation season, when white families drive through Mthatha on their way to the beach, they do

---

[*] Technically, the Xhosa language is isiXhosa, an individual Xhosa is umXhosa, and the Xhosa people are amaXhosa. For simplicity's sake, I have eliminated the noun class prefixes.

so with their windows rolled up, doors locked, and a look on their face that says, "We're not stopping until we get through this town."

Like many cities its size in South Africa or the United States, Mthatha does have crime. The radio was stolen out of my car shortly after my arrival. Another time I returned to the car to find a man unconcernedly picking the lock. When I asked, "Can I help you?" he looked up and nonchalantly began to stroll away. I sighed ruefully. The police were too overstretched investigating successful crimes to have any time to be concerned about this. But Mthatha's reputation is overstated and mostly undeserved. Mthatha is a pretty town, bisected by the Mthatha River, and surrounded by rolling farmland that stretches to the foothills of the Drakensberg escarpment in the north and down to the Indian Ocean in the south.

It is also a rapidly growing place. As South Africans have had more freedom to move since the end of apartheid, more and more people have chosen to move to urban areas in search of economic opportunity. In the Transkei, this means people are leaving the "rural areas," the catch-all term for the many remote villages in the far reaches of the region, to come to Mthatha in search of work, either in the formal economy or, more likely, in the informal economy of fruit stands, hawkers, and casual labor that pervades the city. In Mthatha, this has translated into new neighborhoods sprouting around town and ever-growing city limits. The sidewalks are overwhelmed with street vendors and foot traffic. Construction seems a constant, as more stores and banks open to cater to the growing population.

The results of this growth are most evident on the city's roads, clogged with more cars than they were designed for. The minibus taxis that are a staple of life in sub-Saharan Africa career everywhere jammed full with passengers. Side alleys and delivery zones that were once set aside for loading and unloading goods have been built on. This forces trucks to deliver their goods while parked in a side lane of a main street, blocking traffic. The national highway connecting Cape Town and Durban passes directly through town, meaning long-haul trucks frequently jam up major intersections. The stoplights work sporadically, pedestrians cross freely and without concern for signals or crosswalks, and lane markings seem mostly to be a suggestion, rarely followed.

Though Mthatha may provide more economic opportunity than the villages, it is a community that is still far distant—in every sense of the word—from the highly developed parts of South Africa, like Cape Town or Johannesburg. A visit to parts of Cape Town feels like a visit to San Francisco, a first-class, first-world city. A village in the rural Transkei has nothing in common with that gleaming way of life. The legacy of years of independence and underdevelopment sits heavy on Mthatha. Socioeconomic indicators are among the worst in the country—higher unemployment, higher infant mortality, and a higher HIV prevalence rate to name just a few.

Despite this, there were reasons for hope in Mthatha. New stores— especially supermarkets—opened all the time and there was clearly money to support their continued existence. As a regional hub, Mthatha has a university and a new hospital that attracts expatriate African doctors and professors. These high-paid positions and a growing middle class of black South Africans meant there were neighborhoods of large houses in Mthatha and multiple spotless Mercedes on the roads jostling for space with packed minibus taxis. Driving through town, one would see not only bedraggled and unkempt people begging on the side of the road but men in suits and ties and women in spotless traditional garb as well. Much like the rest of South Africa, Mthatha embodies the complexities and contradictions of a people who are struggling to move forward after generations of discrimination and neglect. It was this town that I had pledged to be a part of for the next year.

When I stepped out of the *bakkie* and into the Itipini Community Project on that first day, the full weight of what I was doing finally settled on me. Here I was, a white man in black Africa. I was stepping into a role that had been filled by so many men over the generations. That legacy—and the legacy of the word *mission*—made me feel uneasy, no matter my professed and eager desire to serve others and save people in Itipini.

I was still struggling to determine the significance—if any—of mission to a person of my globally minded, equality-seeking generation. There were the obvious humanitarian and development needs I wanted to involve myself in. But the overall idea I had been rolling around as the basis for my then-nascent approach to mission centered on the idea of incarnational ministry. In the incarnation, God in the form of Jesus crossed the hitherto impassable barrier that marked the divine and human realms as different, separate, and apart and chose to share an existence with humans. It was from this first decision—a decision to give up power and become vulnerable—that God in Jesus was able to teach, heal, and ultimately die and rise again. The reconciling moment of the resurrection was impossible without the incarnational moment celebrated each Christmas. If Jesus saved the world by first being incarnate, my saving mission, on a much more limited scale, had to begin by learning about and sharing parts of life in Itipini. It was incomplete incarnation, to be sure—I was living in a thatch-roofed, mud-brick house on the other side of town, not Itipini, and a yearlong commitment was short, both in mission terms and compared to Jesus' life span—but a barrier was still being crossed.

Christians are supposed to pattern their lives on Christ's but it still made me uncomfortable to compare myself so closely to Jesus. But I did have that modest messiah complex and the analogy to the incarnation was undeniable. By choosing to work in Itipini—a part of the country that most white people avoided and few foreigners ever saw—I was crossing a giant barrier, a barrier characterized by vast differences of race, language, wealth, and—especially—power. When I stepped out of the back of the *bakkie* that first day in Itipini, it was the beginning of my existence-sharing with the people of Itipini. It was the beginning of my vulnerability.

Looking around, I was immediately overwhelmed. Pigs, chickens, and stray, mangy, and often crippled dogs wandered through the Community Project area along with adults and barefoot children, running oblivious to the broken glass scattered seemingly everywhere. Flies glommed on to young children, who seemed so used to them that they barely paid them any mind or even chased them away with their hands. There were few trees and when the sun got high in the sky, even on that late-winter day, there was no place for refuge from the heat. Underneath it all ran the sounds of daily life—neighbors greeting one another, a wash bucket being emptied, two women chatting as they waited at the water tap, the squeaky wheel of a man pushing his cart into town.

Gazing over Itipini, I saw the hundreds of shacks, each unique, each created by a particular combination of whatever materials had been available at the time. There were the tiny, one-room shacks that barely stood up, the kind used by the transient part of the population. These were people who came in from the rural areas in hopes of finding work or to visit a sick relative. But I also saw larger shacks that I would later learn had several rooms, many a warren of passageways and hidden corners connecting an eating and living area with bedrooms. These had clean floors with dirt that had been so trodden down it had taken on a compacted, almost concrete-like feel. These shacks belonged to the more established families, many of whom had been in Itipini for decades, and had more of the comforts of home. Old televisions and radios run off of old car batteries were particularly popular.

Looking closer at hand, I saw the buildings of the Itipini Community Project. In the early 1990s, a few expatriate women and a few local men began coming to Itipini to provide primary medical care and a few programs for the children of the community. One of these women was Jenny McConnachie, an Episcopal missionary who had been living in Mthatha for a decade by that point with her husband, Chris, an orthopedic surgeon who was in charge of a local hospital. Over time, as others moved away, Jenny—a slight woman well past retirement age in any country I knew of but looking and acting twenty years younger—came to be responsible for the ongoing projects in Itipini. She and Chris were able to finance the work through African Medical Mission, a nongovernmental organization they had previously established to support Chris' work.

By the time I arrived in Itipini, the Community Project had grown substantially since its early days. As I turned and looked around I could see each small building, built when the money had been available, that housed a different program. The low-slung, wooden clinic was still the core of the Project. But on the far side of the Project area was the rainbow-painted, two-room cinder block preschool. Closer by were the three spaces that formed the nucleus of the after-school program: an activities room, a weight room, and two shipping containers that had once housed the clinic but now were used for a wide variety of after-school programs and meetings. Off to my right was the small kitchen and pantry area. Lunch was prepared there for the preschool children and food was distributed as part of a nutrition program for patients with HIV or tuberculosis. Except for Jenny—and now me—all of it was operated by about a dozen local staff.

But it was what I couldn't immediately see that marked the greatest differences. The cruelties imposed by a life of extreme poverty are often hidden. Hunger, for instance, is not readily visible. The government's extensive—and, for Africa, unusual—program of social grants meant most people were minimally fed. I never saw anything resembling the pictures of malnourished children with distended bellies and falling-out hair that seem to be a staple of Western media coverage of Africa. But hunger made itself known in subtler ways. I had brought some food with me to tide me through lunchtime but I realized at once that it was a mistake. I could never bring myself to eat an apple in front of children who just looked at me with longing eyes when they saw it. One day, when some children saw a bag of bananas in my car, they asked for them with a relentlessness and desperation that surprised me because they hadn't "looked" hungry. No one was going to bed with the contented and full feeling I routinely did.

In that first week, a woman who had severely twisted her ankle came into the clinic for treatment. The treatment struck me as obvious—ice the ankle and stay off it for a few days. But without electricity, she didn't have any ice. As a woman with numerous responsibilities just to keep her household running—collecting water and firewood, cooking, keeping track of children—she didn't have the luxury of staying off the ankle. I got one or two ice packs from our propane-fueled fridge and propped her in a corner for fifteen minutes. Then I wrapped her ankle as tightly as I could, gave her a painkiller, and sent her out the door. "Staying off it" is not an option when you live in a place like Itipini.

A lifetime of injuries like these, compounded by intense physical exertion every single day, meant pain became another invisible factor of life in Itipini. It was remarkable what people—particularly the women—subjected themselves to on a daily basis. I routinely saw women carrying bucket after bucket of water, forty to fifty pounds each, countless times every day. When I tried, I could barely manage to carry a twenty-pound bucket a few feet before the crushing pain in my neck and spine made me stop. Without facilities I took for granted—running water, heat, sewer, and so on—life was much more arduous. When you added a lifetime of hard labor just to survive and a few injuries that never had the time to heal properly, it made for a difficult existence. One of the most requested medications at the clinic was methyl salicylate ointment—"rubbing stuff" as patients called it—that was supposed to relax muscles and heal pain. Our patients swore by its evergreen-scented healing properties.

Life was not easy inside those shacks I only saw from a distance. No one chooses to live in an informal community. The local government and police preferred to keep places like Itipini at arm's length. It was impossible to find a social worker willing to make a house call to a family, and the only time the police came to visit was when they were in search of prison escapees or stolen goods. Itipini was a good place to hide both. After the sun set, the informal relationship the government had with the community became clear. Physical and sexual violence could happen unchecked by law. We saw its results in the morning in the clinic.

Scattered amid that sea of shacks was a string of *shebeens,* unlicensed bars that sold beer and homebrew to a familiar roster of clients. Homebrew—occasionally spiked with acid from the old batteries to give it an extra kick—was common, but the most popular drink was Juba, a beer that came in a one-liter, milk carton-like container, and sold for approximately fifty cents. Crates and crates of these cartons were wheeled into the community every day, and old containers featuring, incongruously, a red pineapple logo, were common in the piles of trash around the area. Indeed, at least one shack was made almost entirely from such cartons. Gin was another drink of choice, so popular that many of the containers that patients brought to the clinic for their medication were empty gin bottles. Alcohol has the same effects in Itipini that I recognized from my time riding in the back of an ambulance. Soon after I arrived in Itipini, a young man was hurriedly carried into the clinic with fresh gunshot wounds in his abdomen and his elbow. All involved were drunk. We got him to the hospital and he survived, but it was one of many similar alcohol-fueled episodes I would encounter.

These obvious hardships—some external and structural, others self-imposed—defined the contours of life in Itipini. They were what I needed to learn about if I truly wanted to share an existence with these people. But what struck me vividly on that first day was that despite the circumstances, the people in Itipini were an impressive lot. As I watched them swirl around me, it was clear they led their lives with a pride that belied their circumstances. They smiled and laughed and joked with one another. They sang and prayed together. They welcomed visitors, including me. Many children who showed up at preschool appeared with shiny smiles in impressively clean clothes. They fought and cried and shared and played like children anywhere. If the word *dignity* has not been too degraded, I would use it to describe how people in Itipini could still hold their heads high and lead their lives as best as they could, despite the poverty and despair that surrounded them every day.

That first day, bearing up under an overwhelming sensory overload—new sights, smells, sounds, animals, peoples—but wanting so deeply to become a part of this life, I struggled to find my bearings as the workday swung into action around me. Some staff members were unloading food from the *bakkie*. Others were preparing for the day in the preschool. A few hopeful souls were already approaching Jenny for care. It was the beginning of a well-established rhythm. By the time I figured out how I could be helpful, it was time for the morning community prayers under the veranda in the middle of the Project. The preschool children and women gathered around. Some looked distracted, others tired, and a few impatient for prayers to be over. But all joined their strong voices in song. I stood on the edge, listening and trying to be unobtrusive. Tentative though I was, I was grateful to be welcomed into this circle. For them, it was the beginning of one more day like any other. For me, it was the beginning of something profoundly unlike anything I had ever experienced. Vulnerability began here.

Three

A Weak Tongue

WHEN I STEPPED OUT of the *bakkie* that first day in Itipini, I was immediately greeted by a woman passing by on her way to the tap. Of course, at the time, I didn't realize that's what she was doing.

"Molo," she said. I looked around in confusion. She pressed on. "Unjani?" she inquired.

This was embarrassing. She was obviously trying to be friendly but I had no idea that she was greeting me with what I would later learn is the all-purpose Xhosa word for "hello" and then asking how I was.

I wanted to say, "There's been some mistake. I only speak English. Don't you?" Even before the thought was fully formulated, I realized both how hopelessly American it sounded and how little I had done to prepare for this language barrier.

I stood there looking confused as the woman waited expectantly for a reply. I looked around for someone to help. Jenny was already into the swing of things with the workday. Even if she wasn't busy, she wouldn't be able to spend all her energy translating every little interaction for me. I smiled at my new acquaintance, blushed, and tried to walk away, only to be greeted with another "molo" from another passing woman.

Thoughts of saving Africa went right out of my head. At this point, I would settle simply for greeting Africans.

The single, dominant, and overriding factor affecting all my interactions in Itipini on that first day and in all my early days, weeks, and months was the gargantuan language barrier that stood between the people in Itipini and me. People spoke Xhosa to each other and Xhosa to me. I was adrift in a sea of Xhosa, not a word of which I understood. I could almost see the barrier in my imagination. It was dark and tall, stretching up to the heavens, and standing firmly between me and whomever I was trying to speak with. Sometimes I personified it, imagining a sneering face that mocked me and my futile attempts to scramble over, under, around, or through it.

The truth was I was hopelessly unprepared. YASC missionaries receive a language training stipend but when I had learned about this during mission training, I had confidently thought to myself, "They speak English in South Africa. I won't need to use that money." Never have I been so thoroughly and comprehensively wrong in my life.

I persisted in this vain belief even though I had been forewarned that South Africa has eleven official languages and Xhosa is widespread in Mthatha. I had even met my predecessor, who had impressed me with her Xhosa and impressed upon me the fact that if I wanted to communicate with people in Itipini, I would have to learn Xhosa. In those few months of transition, in the weeks of eager anticipation, I had banished all thought of language differences from my mind. When I let myself get nervous, I focused my anxieties on the thought that I would have to learn to drive on the left-hand side of the road. That proved to be a cakewalk compared to learning Xhosa.

I had actually been exposed to Xhosa prior to my arrival in South Africa. A few years earlier, I had worked with a South African at summer camp who had entertained us by speaking his native language. What we really liked was when he demonstrated words that had clicking noises in them. So fascinated was I by those clicks that on several occasions I had him try to teach me how to make them myself. It was difficult and I had other responsibilities so I quickly gave up trying, confident in the knowledge that it would never be of any use to me in my life. It came as something of a shock—and a sign of divine irony—that the language that was now causing me so much consternation was the same language I had once so blithely dismissed.

Xhosa was the first language in which I was seriously trying to gain verbal fluency. In order to learn it, I realized, I had to be willing to try to speak it and make mistake after mistake in front of native speakers. I am used to being a quick study. Making mistakes doesn't come easily to me. People were going to laugh at me. They were going to correct me and point out all my mistakes. I didn't want to try anything until I had mastered it, but I couldn't know I had mastered anything until I tried it out on a native speaker. It was a constant battle with my pride.

The click consonants didn't help. There are three distinct clicks, represented by the letters c, q, and x, though the sounds have no relation to how those letters are pronounced in English. I found all of them difficult, particularly the x-click, which took me close to ten months even to approximate. Without the x, I couldn't even properly pronounce the name of the language I was trying to speak or the people whose existence I was ostensibly seeking to share. Even with the c- and q-clicks, which were easier, it was difficult to insert them into words. Then when they were combined with other letters to form diphthongs and triphthongs, it became nearly impossible.

I eventually found a superb private tutor, but my first Xhosa teacher was a six-year-old preschool student named Vela. I had hoped the children who were always around could help me expand my vocabulary. I would point at an object, name it in English, and hope they would tell me the Xhosa word. But when I said the English word most of them repeated it after me. When I said plaintively, "No, in Xhosa," they laughed and repeated how I had mispronounced "Xhosa." (Due to my struggles with the x-click, I made a noise more closely approximating the q-click. What would come out is qosa, which is nonsense.)

But Vela understood what I wanted. When I pointed to my elbow and said, "elbow," he pointed to his and said, "elbow—ingqiniba." Later, he pointed at himself and said, "Vela," and then at me. I pointed at myself and said, "Jesse." He repeated it, rolling the strange-sounding word around in his mouth so that it came out more like "Jesses." Most importantly, Vela pointed out how I messed up. In the word for elbow, the q-click is made by putting the bottom of the tongue against the top of the mouth and then bringing it down. Vela, of course, did it effortlessly but I would strain so hard the tendons on my neck stood out. Vela noticed this and kept pointing to my throat. I didn't understand at first but I finally realized what he was trying to communicate. I didn't have to try so hard and didn't have to make my clicks so pronounced. When I finally pronounced a word correctly, he gave a nod of approval that I began to crave. It was a businesslike nod as if to say, "great, got that one, let's move on."

I soon became eager to try out my Xhosa on anyone who would listen. Driving home one day, I greeted a hitchhiker with my best *molo* and *unjani*. She was surprised to hear a white man speak Xhosa and complimented me on my skill. I demurred and protested about the difficulty of the clicks, demonstrating my inability to make the x-sound properly. "You know why you can't speak Xhosa?" she said. "It is because you have a weak tongue. We Xhosas are born with strong tongues!" She demonstrated a resounding x-click. I was jealous. How could I learn a language if my anatomy prejudiced me against it?

Still, I did not lose sight of the importance of learning Xhosa. I would certainly be of more use to Jenny if I could minimally inquire about a patient's health. I wanted—deeply!—to learn more about the experience of people in Itipini, and there was no way they could share that with me in English. I couldn't begin to be a part of the community if I couldn't even greet someone on her way to the water faucet.

More than that, by attempting to speak Xhosa, however imperfectly, I was lessening in some small way the power differential that existed between me—relatively wealthy, educated, and mobile—and the people in Itipini. Simply by choosing to speak in their language—and make countless errors—I gave them power by making them the experts in the conversation. It was this realization that helped me wrestle my pride and keep trying—and messing up—in Xhosa.

In my first weeks in Itipini, it was to the clinic that I turned my attention and my time. The small wooden building about thirty feet long and ten feet wide was the focal point of the Community Project. Its schedule determined the rhythm of the workday and the pattern of the week. More than that, being in the clinic meant being close to Jenny, a security blanket of sorts. I wasn't about to venture alone into the big unknown of Itipini. Jenny, I reasoned, would be able to find something for me to do.

Jenny is a woman of irrepressible energy and good spirits and the driving force behind the clinic. She saw patients throughout the morning and into the afternoon, smoothly pivoting from the woman with perpetually sore knees to the child with a cut foot to the infant with diarrhea, all the while fending off drunk patients, the occasional request for money, and men—always the men—who wanted to cut in line. She paused only to refill her coffee cup.

Across from Jenny was Dorothy, a retired nurse and native of the Mthatha area. Slower, quieter, and more stolid than Jenny, Dorothy was immediately intimidating to me. She had the sort of crustiness that is the prerogative of a retired nurse in South Africa. She also had precious little patience for young white volunteers who couldn't speak Xhosa but wanted so much to help. She rightly saw people like me as getting in the way. Only after it was clear I would be staying a while and that I could do more than just greet people in Xhosa did she open up to me, revealing a deep tenderness and concern for the patients we saw.

The variety of ailments that prompted patients to seek care was stunning—older women with aches and pains; schoolchildren with headaches and sore throats; women young and old looking for birth control; men and women complaining about sexually transmitted infections; patients dying of AIDS, unable to walk and carried into the clinic on a stretcher. While there were a few curtains that could be rearranged to cordon off certain areas and create some semblance of privacy, for the most part, the clinic was just one big room, with people flowing in and out of the door all day long.

I had imagined that with my medical background, I might be able to transcend the language barrier and help someone somehow. With all the broken glass and rusting metal around, there were lots of wounds to bandage, and this was something I could easily do. But beyond concerns that were visibly obvious, if I couldn't speak Xhosa, I couldn't figure out why a patient had come to the clinic. I had to rely on Jenny to figure it out for me and that only made me a burden to her.

As a result, most of my time was spent with a series of decidedly unglamorous jobs. The pills we distributed came in bottles of one thousand or five thousand but we distributed them only in bags of eight or fifteen or twenty-eight. I spent countless hours counting pills into little bags. Counting pills was not exactly what I had had in mind when I resolved to move to Africa, and I frequently had to remind myself of the importance of the task. HIV patients, for instance, needed the multivitamin cocktails—at 150 pills, the worst one to count—to maintain the strength of their immune system. The job involved almost no interaction with anyone else—in fact, interaction was awful, as it made you lose count—but it was important nonetheless.

Patients' health records were kept on index cards in a series of drawers against one wall. When patients came in and sat on the bench to wait, it was my job to find their card so they'd be ready when Dorothy or Jenny came available. It seemed like a straightforward enough job, and it even involved interacting with and getting to know people. It might even have been easy if the names were in English. But the language barrier reared its mocking head again. When I asked a patient her name, it rolled off her tongue so quickly I could barely tell what was the first name and what the surname. At the time, Xhosa names all seemed to be a minimum of eight syllables long and to start with either M or N. Many names had clicks so I had to decide if it was an x-, a c-, or a q-click (and if it was a diphthong, like gc) and insert that into my mental spelling of the name. I had shown up so full of enthusiasm and was unable to do something as easy as find medical records. Fortunately, most of the patients were, well, patient with my efforts, and some of the younger ones could even write their names down. Still, Agnes Jon and Elizabeth Williams were always my favorite patients.

Some of the records dated to the mid-1990s, a series of dog-eared, stained, and ragged index cards, stapled together again and again then held together with a rubber band when they became too thick for staples. The stories told in these cards were fascinating. There were the older women, often only in their late forties or early fifties but looking twenty or thirty years older, who would come in frequently for pain-killers, so worn down were they by the collected decades of carrying water, cooking food, washing laundry, and chasing their children and now their children's children. There were young mothers, many several years younger than me, whose cards dated to when they were four or five. Their records stretched from the cuts, scrapes, and stomachaches of childhood through to a positive pregnancy test and into notes about breast-feeding or a sore back that came from carrying the child.

It was these young mothers who gave me the first indications that I was settling in to Itipini and moving beyond the language barrier. Tuesday was baby clinic day, the day to distribute baby food and, for the HIV-positive mothers, formula replacement for those who couldn't breast-feed. The food and formula were the hook to draw the mothers in so that Jenny and Dorothy could check on the health of the babies and ensure their immunizations were up-to-date. It also allowed them to check on the health of the mothers and the baby's older siblings. We could easily see sixty or eighty patients on a Tuesday, far more than the non-Tuesday average of thirty-five to forty. It was also the most hectic day of the week, with children crawling, drooling, toddling, screaming, crying, and laughing while mothers talked and jostled for position in line. When we arrived on Tuesdays, there was already a line outside the door, and it never seemed to slacken during the day.

The long and slow line meant there was plenty of time to spend with these young women as they waited. At first, I was too unknown for them to engage me, and I was too unsure of myself to do anything beyond find their cards. But as word began to spread that I was the new Anne—my YASC predecessor, who had left two months prior to my arrival—more people began to recognize me and I noticed a change in how many of the young mothers reacted to me. While the missionary is not traditionally seen as a sexy figure, the young mothers were flirting with me.

Of course, everything they said was in Xhosa. But it turned out that many things are universal: embarrassed giggles, blushing faces, and shy smiles, helped along by the occasional question in halting English—"What is your name?" or "How old are you?" I am not normally very suave or sure of myself around the opposite sex. Responding to such advances in English would have given me trouble enough. But in Xhosa it was even harder. All I could manage was "hello, how are you, I'm fine" and "my name is Jesse." So I simply returned the smiles and played with the babies, which only excited more giggles and whispers—not that I would have been able to understand them even if they weren't whispering.

Sometimes when I felt particularly chivalrous, I'd start speaking to everyone in French as if to prove I could speak a little bit of another language. This mostly consisted of calling everyone "mademoiselle" and saying "oui" a lot, and it wasn't clear they even recognized that I was speaking a different language. When I was feeling mischievous and weighing a patient, I'd secretly step on the scale or hold onto the weight to make them seem heavier than they were. But I learned a woman's weight doesn't hold quite the same importance in Itipini as it does in the United States. The women just looked at me, wondering why it was taking so long for me to weigh them.

Our lives were in stark contrast. Their medical records told stories of pregnancy, assault, and HIV. If my medical records had been on hand, they would have shown nothing worse than a few cases of strep throat and a broken leg from a sledding accident. But our flirtatious interactions showed me we had a common core as we played more or less the same games people our age play all over the world every day.

What with the flirting and never-ending line of patients, Tuesdays provided me plenty to do. But there were four other days of the week, and so I began to concentrate on the patients with tuberculosis. The horrible symptoms of TB—coughing, little appetite, sweating at night, general weakness—meant most patients were eager to begin the six to eight months of daily pills and occasional injections to cure it. For most patients, it was no trouble to get them to take the first two months of pills. Their health would improve markedly and reasonably quickly. Rereading the medical records of discharged patients, I often marveled at how patients had progressed from such dire remarks about their health several months earlier to a relatively robust and active health at the time of discharge.

The challenge was getting patients to complete the full course of treatment. Many patients would be faithful for the first few months of treatment and then stop coming, convinced that they were cured and not understanding that the remaining TB in their lungs was mutating and becoming drug resistant or spreading to other organs in their body. The result of this challenge is a system in use around the world called Directly Observed Therapy, and the clinic was a D.O.T. site. The patients had to come to the clinic, and we had to watch them take their medication. I ticked off each day on our charts and made sure their pillboxes, which we kept in empty plastic ice cream containers, were full when they arrived.

The patients who occupied most of my attention were the ones who stopped showing up before they were finished. I became a TB-pill truant officer, hunting down patients to try to convince them—in my limited and very fractured Xhosa—to keep coming to the clinic every single day. When I spotted the truant men in town, pushing their carts looking for work, I shouted to them over the traffic, imploring them to come to the clinic to get their medicine. Generally, these patients were impressed that someone was showing such interest in them and would return for their pills for a few weeks before backsliding, making me start the whole process over again. I liked it, though, and I liked the patients. It was something I could do. And because I saw them every day, these patients—along with the young mothers—were my first "friends" in Itipini, people like Fumanekile, whom I could pick out from the crowd easiest.

Most TB patients were older. The TB had preyed on their compromised and aging immune systems. But one patient stood out. Siphisihle was six years old and a quiet, diffident student in the preschool. Ideally, she would stop in the clinic every day for her pills, I'd mash them up and mix them with some multivitamin syrup so she could drink them rather than swallow them whole, and she'd head out the door to our morning prayers. But her attendance was sporadic and many of her pills sat unclaimed day after day. When I checked in the preschool, I learned her attendance was sporadic there as well, so she wasn't just skipping by us on her way to school.

I asked around about her and one of the preschool teachers suggested I visit her at home. I paused. I wanted Siphisihle to finish her treatment, but I had rarely been out of the confines of the cluster of our community center and never on my own. Summoning my courage, I went to find her.

The shack Siphisihle shared with her family was not large—a rough square maybe twelve feet on a side and made out of the usual array of tarps, metal, old car parts, and branches that characterized the homes in Itipini. It was surrounded by the usual mud and detritus that engulfed the community. A few pigs wandered nearby, nosing around for scraps and a stray dog limped along a nearby path. Siphisihle herself along with her three older siblings were casually playing around the shack, oblivious to the fact that she could be in preschool at that very moment. Her father, I knew, was absent and there was no sign of her mother, whom I later learned spent most of her days in town trying to earn money but more often passed the time outside a local liquor store. In these circumstances—four siblings under twelve and on their own—it was no wonder that Siphisihle was missing her TB treatment. There was no one at home to make sure that she went to school every day and no one to emphasize the importance of taking the pills.

There was much that was wrong with the situation and I wanted to solve it all, all at once. But focusing on what I could do, I greeted the children, used the Xhosa word for medicine, and offered my hand to

Siphisihle. There was a shy smile on her face as we walked back to the clinic, and she seemed happy to be shown some attention. I mashed up the pills and sent her on to preschool. She was late but would at least be in time for lunch and the afternoon snack.

She didn't show up the next day. I returned to her shack, again offered my hand, and again mashed up the pills and sent her on her way. This went on every day for a week, my confidence of my place in Itipini growing as the two of us walked hand-in-hand through the mud and garbage and past the tumbledown shacks to the clinic and then on to the preschool.

One day, as we were opening the clinic, I turned to see Siphisihle standing in the doorway, knowing she should be there but too shy to ask for her pills. I smiled and prepared the mashed-up pill concoction for her. The next day she was there as well. And then the next. And the next.

I wasn't fluent in Xhosa. I still couldn't find patients' cards. I was still more of a hindrance than a help. I hadn't really "saved" anyone. But as I watched Siphisihle graduate from preschool that December just a few days after she finished her treatment and tested negative for TB, I realized the barriers that so defined my first few weeks and months in Itipini were—ever so slightly—beginning to crumble.

Four

The Saints Go Dancing In

STEPPING OUT OF THE clinic for a breath of fresh air one afternoon, I noticed a cluster of children intently staring at something underneath the playground. I wandered over to see what was happening. One child in the middle of the group was holding a dead rat by its tail. Another had apparently decided to turn it into a biology project, as the rat was partially torn apart and its innards were sort of falling out. My Xhosa wasn't good enough to tell them to put it down but the horrified look on my face and my strangled gulp must have communicated the message clearly enough. They ran off but returned after I looked away.

Aside from their occasional forays in biology, the children were irresistible. Their large and tender smiles and loads of energy drew me in. With the (admittedly large) exception of their first language and upbringing, these children were not much different from the children I had known as a Sunday school teacher or camp counselor. They played and argued and cried and ran around like children I knew in North America. And they were always around. The noise and energy of the preschool was a constant background hum to our work in the clinic. When they moved to the outdoor veranda for lunch it became much more than a hum.

Ncediwe and Nthatisi, the preschool teachers, were kindhearted and good women who had the potential to be great teachers. But they were also overstretched mothers, caregivers, and entrepreneurs. By the time they showed up for work, they were tired from the daily grind of life. It was easy for their lessons to be abbreviated and for the preschool to descend into loosely supervised playtime for the children. Still, even this was better than having the children stay at home. In the preschool, they had clean floors and toys that none of them had at home. And there was always lunch, which in my mind by itself justified the existence of the preschool, not to mention the toothbrushing and daily vitamins that went with it.

I began to join the preschool lessons, hanging back and trying to be helpful around the margins. I sat with them as they learned about how plants grew. I listened as they learned the letters of the alphabet and took turns writing them on the chalkboard. I watched as they divided into groups and went to different corners of the classroom to play with the donated toys. Learning was happening, no small feat in a community where the press of daily tasks usually overwhelmed any effort at anything beyond that which was necessary for survival.

But I was hardly satisfied. The trouble, I realized, was that I still wasn't *doing* anything. I had come all this way, intent on making a difference, on helping out, and—though I didn't always acknowledge it to myself—on saving these people in Itipini. And what could I do? The Project seemed to run fine without me and the language barrier meant I still struggled to answer a child's question about the ABCs.

As I sat down with my journal one evening, I realized something new. I wrote, "In this year I will need to shift my focus from *doing* to *being*. In Alaska, my focus was on the former: how many news stories could I write, ambulance runs could I take, etc. Now I need to realize that perhaps the greatest gift I can give right now is that of a loving and supportive presence. I won't be able to quantify the results of my work. I am not at peace with this." The Western, results-oriented culture was a deeply written part of my identity. But I had reached a place where I was no longer as able as I am in my own culture. Though I could acknowledge to my journal that who I could *be* in Itipini was more important than what I could *do*, it took many months before I could even begin to be a little comfortable with the idea.

The implicit belief underlying my new conviction about the importance of being and not doing was that somehow being a loving and supportive presence is easy. It isn't.

Attendance varied at the preschool, depending on the weather, what time of month it was, and a whole host of other factors I never fully understood, but there were routinely between thirty and fifty children. When I went to the preschool, it seemed that every last one of them wanted a part of me. I was besieged by children doing anything to get my attention. This ranged from the cute and endearing, like shouting my name or smiling shyly at me, to the aggravating and painful, like hitting me, jumping on me, using my shirt to scale me like a rock face, and, my least favorite, tugging my hair, sometimes so hard it jerked my head back.

I tried to get to know the children individually or in small groups, sitting with a few at a time or being with a handful on the playground. But the decision about who got my attention—even in short spurts—provoked giant battles. I learned to rotate among children as frequently as possible. But even that didn't resolve things. One day, while sitting on the playground with a group of children and trying to expand my Xhosa vocabulary, I rotated the children who sat in my lap. But one child was so disappointed when his turn was over that he kept trying to climb back on. I tried as patiently as I could to communicate the idea that his turn was over. But he didn't understand or didn't want to. Seeing that his attempts to climb back on me were futile, he climbed to the next level of the playground above where I was sitting and let a big gob of saliva fall down on me. I beat a hasty retreat to the clinic.

It was understandable to me that these children wanted attention from a grown-up figure, especially one who was tall and white and male and new to Itipini. While some students did show up in the morning clean and well dressed, many were so thoroughly ignored by their parents, relatives, and anyone and everyone else that they were desperate for anything they could get. They had been given so little to begin with. If I could build them up a little bit just by spending time with them, I wanted to. They swarmed around the car in the morning when I arrived and chased after me as I drove away in the afternoon. There was little respite.

As if to mock my messiah complex, which had more or less gone into hiatus the moment I first heard someone speak Xhosa, the students stumbled over my unusual name. Their best efforts to say "Jesse" came out as "Jesu," the Xhosa name for Jesus. "Jesu!" they cried when they saw me, trying to get my attention. As my vocabulary expanded, I wrote a little song: "Jesus is in heaven. Jesse is on earth." That helped them learn the difference but many still struggled, adding, as Vela had, a third *s* and calling me "Jesses."

Matthew's Gospel records Jesus telling his followers, "Let the little children come to me, and do not stop them." I had always appreciated Jesus' child-centered focus. But after a few weeks with the preschoolers at Itipini, I realized what Jesus is saying is not always as easy and cute as I had previously thought. In fact, it is downright difficult at times. (The passage goes on to say, "and he laid his hands on them and went on his way." I wanted to know how I was supposed to go on my way when I had three children clinging to each leg.) Another translation of this passage is "suffer the little children." Suffer them I did. I wasn't enjoying my time with them at all.

I tried to improve the situation. I learned the Xhosa word for "stop" and would use it when a child was particularly vigorous in his attempt to yank my hair out or punch me. But when I tried to speak to one child about his behavior in my "stern voice"—admittedly, something that has always been more comical than effective for me—he would just laugh and smile, so happy to finally be getting the very attention he craved, even if it was negative. While I spoke with the one child, five others were punching and tugging at me in search of that same slice of attention.

I also knew the Xhosa word for "no"—"hayi." Sometimes when the children hit me, I responded with a stern glare and "hayi." I was surprised that when I did this, the child would turn and cower, as if expecting me to hit him or her. But my hands were not raised—they were too busy holding another child—and when I didn't hit the child, he would turn, smile, and start hitting me again. What I really wanted to do was explain that violence wasn't a good answer. But there were too many situations and I lacked the vocabulary to express so complex a thought.

Nothing I was doing seemed to be very effective. I was the pre-school punching bag. I was a distraction when I went to the preschool. I was still too much in demand and I didn't know how to control a crowd of children in another language. And it made me angry. There was only so much pushing and prodding and pulling that I could tolerate. Their perfectly understandable inability to understand my instructions and my own, also understandable, inability to communicate this message effectively made me so frustrated I wanted to lash out at the children.

At our mission training, we had discussed the challenge of, in the words of Desmond Tutu, "sharing grace gracefully." We discussed this in the context of sharing the challenging and occasionally confrontational message of the Bible in a way that also respects and embraces the local context. It surprised me that this challenge cropped up in my interactions with the children. My aggravation would mount much faster than I was used to with children and led me to act remarkably ungracefully. Occasionally, I used the roof of one of our small buildings as a time-out zone. I could hoist the children up there and let them stew in their own juices for a few minutes and they couldn't get down. But it was an unsatisfying option. I couldn't explain why I had put them on the roof and the look of terror on their faces at being so far off the ground usually made me bring them down quickly.

I tried to remind myself that the children were not the ones I needed to be directing my aggravation at. There were larger targets, like absent parents or the conditions these children were forced to live in that should have been the real sources of my frustration. But it was hard to get angry at absent or amorphous entities when there was a child pulling my hair for attention. Stymied in the preschool, I often found it necessary to withdraw to the relative safety of the clinic where the children seemed to know not to go. I was back where I began and no closer to making any kind of difference, much less saving a single person.

🖎

If only, I thought, I could figure out a way to turn this mess of eager, energetic, and overwhelming children into a slightly more orderly mob, perhaps we could all get along a bit better. The overriding goal was to channel my time with the children into something productive that could involve them all equally. That the children could sing I knew from listening to their morning prayers. So could I. It seemed only a small matter that we knew how to sing in different languages. After several weeks of finding myself frustrated by the children, I brought my guitar along with me one morning.

After prayers I came into the preschool strumming the guitar. Instantly, I was transformed. Instead of swarming around me, they pointed and whispered to one another, saying "isiginci," which I learned to be the Xhosa word for guitar. A sort of reverent hush—as quiet as any group of preschoolers could be—fell over them as they waited to see what I would do next.

On the drive in, I had decided to try "When the Saints Go Marching In" as our first number. The chorus, I thought, was pretty straightforward, and we could repeat it until they got the hang of it. But a confused look came over their faces when I started teaching them the lyrics. I asked them to repeat after me but they could only sort of mumble a rough imitation of the words. I didn't blame them. I was having a hard enough time learning their language, and most of what I said was a bad imitation of what others around me had said. Undeterred, I started playing and singing, hoping they would join in.

They didn't join in the singing that first time but as soon as I started playing the guitar, a new look came over their faces—one of excitement and joy. They stood up and started dancing to the music. By the tenth or so time that I had played "When the Saints" that morning, only one or two had the hang of the lyrics. But no one was pulling my hair. No one was clinging to my legs. Everyone was moving and grooving and jumping and swaying. It was, I imagine, much like saints marching in heaven.

It was then that I realized I did know a South African song, "Siyahamba" or "We are Marching in the Light of God." The lyrics I learned in the United States were in Zulu and slightly different from how they sing it in Xhosa. But the chords were the same and the children recognized the melody immediately. We launched into a very long rendition of the song in which we not only marched, but also danced, sang, clapped, skipped, jumped, and ran in the light of God.

The next day, I returned with my guitar. The enthusiasm the children showed the day before had not diminished. They continued to dance, and a few more even managed to sing along with "When the Saints." But for many, singing and dancing at the same time was just too big of a challenge. They would dance a bit and then stare at me and then start dancing again. After another lengthy rendition of "Siyahamba," I was ready to leave but Ncediwe and Nthatisi asked for more. Not wanting to teach another song and have the lyrics get confused with "When the Saints," I opted for "Johnny B. Goode." It's not a song whose lyrics I ever expected them to learn, nor was it of a particularly religious nature. But it is a rollicking good time nonetheless, and I had plenty of experience playing it because the theme song of the summer camp I had worked at was set to the same tune. Most importantly, it was a number the children could dance to easily.

It didn't matter that on that day I forgot almost all the words to the second verse, mixed in lyrics from the theme song, missed half the chord changes, and got so winded from dancing that I could barely sing the last chorus. What mattered was that we were singing and dancing and having a constructive time together. When I left the children that morning, for the first time I felt not frustrated or angry but satisfied, relieved, and more than a little bit happy.

My guitar had an unexpected benefit with another important group in Itipini. Later that week, as I walked away from the preschool after another rousing morning sing session, a few of the Community Project employees asked me to play for them as well. They had been cooking in the kitchen and had easily been able to hear me the last few days. I was used to using my guitar to entertain children and it struck me as odd that these women would be interested in it as well. These same women had struck me as so ferociously efficient and capable when I arrived that I had steered clear of their work spaces, afraid of interfering with what seemed like an already smoothly running operation. But they were also the backbone of the Community Project and my coworkers for the next year, so I started strumming "When the Saints," attracting a growing crowd of amused onlookers. When I finished, the women requested "Siyahamba." This time they joined in with me and even began to move their feet a little and shake their hips ever so slightly in an approximation of a dance. Not wanting the moment to end too soon, when we finished "Siyahamba," I launched into another rendition of "Johnny B. Goode," this time sparing nothing, not even the one-legged hop, à la Michael J. Fox in *Back to the Future*, across the Community Project yard and back again. This went over exceedingly well.

I was running out of energy and asked someone to bring me my water bottle. Several of the women asked for a sip as well. It was a hot day and they had been dancing too so I passed my water bottle around. I noticed a few puzzled looks on their faces but didn't think much of it, being too preoccupied with how well the morning had gone.

It wasn't until that afternoon on the drive out of Itipini that Nthatisi laughingly asked me if I had shared my water bottle with the women. I answered I had.

"Do you know what they thought it was?" she asked.

"I assume water. I told them I wanted *amanzi*," using the Xhosa word for water that I had recently learned.

By this point she was beside herself with laughter. "Why do you ask?" I wanted to know.

"They thought it was gin!" she blurted out, between fits of laughter. "They thought the only way you could sing and dance like that is to be drunk! That's why they wanted it!"

An antidrug phrase I had learned in elementary school came to mind—"get high on life." I didn't know how it would translate in Xhosa.

My guitar rapidly became an integral part of my relationship with the preschool children and a tool I used to become part of the community. We couldn't speak the same language but we could sing and dance together and that helped lower other barriers. I continued to bring my guitar to the preschool, not every day, but consistently enough that the children were able to build up a sizable repertoire of English-language songs and I was able to expand my knowledge of Xhosa choruses. When I arrived in the morning, the children would often rush over to check the trunk to see if I had brought the guitar with me. And on days when I hadn't, they would ask, slightly mournfully, "siphi isiginci sakho?"— "where is your guitar?" and make an air guitar motion just in case I didn't understand.

Somehow I was finally doing something. It wasn't, as near as I could tell, saving anyone, but it was something. And playing music with the children lifted my spirits and convinced me it was worthwhile to keep showing up every day in Itipini.

☙

The high point of the school year for the preschool students was the graduation in December, in which the six-year-olds marched across our little stage in caps and gowns we held in storage all year especially for the occasion. It was surprising to see just how many members of the community came out to see the children graduate. The play area in which the students normally ran around now held three or four hundred people, crammed onto benches and peering over the fence. And when a child crossed the stage, his or her mother would often rush out of the crowd and dance in celebration so that the whole community could know her connection to the graduate and share in her joy.

I had been asked to hand out the diplomas to each child, and it was touching to be a part of the ceremony. But as I looked around at many of the older students who had come to see their younger siblings graduate, it occurred to me that for many of these students the preschool graduation was their first and last chance to walk across a stage. The number of obstacles they encountered on the way to graduation from ninth grade—the end of primary school—and then high school were so numerous that I knew only a small handful of these children would ever again have a chance to wear a mortarboard.

At that first preschool graduation, our collective musical knowledge had expanded far enough that I was able to lead some of the young graduates in a rousing rendition of "When the Saints" and "Swing Low, Sweet Chariot," sung simultaneously by two different groups of children. Several women in the crowd started ululating their joy and praise as we sang. On some level, I was becoming part of the community.

Five

"Homeless"

THE PRAYER CIRCLE EACH morning was led by Mkuseli, who had been directing the after-school program for a decade. He was an exceedingly short and slight man, but I was convinced that he grew a few inches and gained a few pounds each morning as he confidently led the group in song and prayer. In other circumstances, he would have made a fine priest. At first, this was all I saw of Mkuseli. The activities he organized for the children, the soccer team he coached, and the youth choir he directed all took place in the afternoon, usually after we closed the clinic. Occasionally, he came into the clinic to refill his coffee partway through the morning and we exchanged greetings but formally and without much emotion. We made a handful of trips into town together to pick up supplies for his programs but they were distant and somewhat formal affairs. He was just turning forty when I arrived and I was a little intimidated by his tenure, knowledge, and seemingly deep immersion in the community. My height meant I towered over him whenever we talked. The intimidation might have run both ways.

Mkuseli's "office" was one of the old shipping containers perched on the edge of the Community Project. On my way past one morning, I heard him singing softly. This was not unusual, as he often sang to himself, usually in Xhosa, and I typically didn't understand. It came as a surprise, therefore, to realize I recognized the lyrics. "Webaba silale maweni, webaba silale maweni," he kept repeating, in the familiar, if unintelligible, opening lines of "Homeless" from Paul Simon's *Graceland*,

41

the album Simon had recorded with several South African musicians. I paused to listen as he tailed off. "I know that song!" I said with a grin on my face.

"Really!" He was surprised.

"Yes, it's Paul Simon and Ladysmith Black Mambazo."

"Oh," he said. "I didn't know."

He had heard the song for the first time the day before on the radio. He liked it so much that it had stayed with him, though he could only remember the opening, repeated lines. He knew of Black Mambazo but not Paul Simon. I explained the connection and promised I would find the song so he could hear it again.

The next day I came to Itipini armed with an iPod. I scrolled around to find "Homeless," showed Mkuseli how to use the earbuds, and pressed play. He was transfixed. When the song was finished, he asked how to play it again. I showed him how to use it and returned to the clinic. Two hours later, I returned. The battery was almost gone, and he had ranged far beyond Paul Simon, ending up somewhere in the realm between Nickel Creek and Joan Jett. There was a huge smile on his face, and he was effusive in his thanks.

The next day I returned not only with my iPod but also a battery-powered pair of speakers and the lyrics to "Homeless." I sat down and insisted he teach me so I could sing along as well. Black Mambazo sings in Zulu, a language closely related to Xhosa, and it was heartening when I read the lyrics to realize I could already translate a few parts of the song. On our first time through I missed most of the clicks and all of the trilling that goes on in the background but, all things considered, it was a fair duet.

I thanked him and got up to return to the clinic. But he stopped me with his arm and said firmly, "Again!" A young woman hanging around the kitchen came over to see what was going on and joined in our second run through the song. A few men loitering nearby came and peeked over my shoulder at the lyrics so they could sing along. Soon, I found myself wishing I had more copies of the lyrics for our growing group. Again and again we sang about being "homeless." I started clicking in the right places. The men were trilling beautifully. I forgot about the line of patients in the clinic and thought only about the radiant look on Mkuseli's face. It was a look, I am sure, that I shared.

Our relationship blossomed at just the right time. It was January, the beginning of the school year in South Africa, and Mkuseli was leading the charge to get the children of Itipini enrolled in the primary school just up the hill. In the week and a half before school started, Mkuseli set out a desk by his container and met with an endless procession of mothers, discussing how they would pay school fees and noting which children needed which uniform parts and in what sizes.

The national and provincial governments were always making hopeful noises about fee-free education. At one point, the principal of the primary school received a letter from the Department of Education informing him that his school had been designated fee-free. But there was no information forthcoming—ever—about how he was to make up the revenue shortfall if he stopped charging fees. He continued to insist on collecting money from students before they could attend school. The fees were about ten to fifteen US dollars a year, but even such a modest fee, especially when combined with the cost of the uniform, could effectively put education out of reach for families earning only a few dollars a day.

The system of social grants was supposed to help alleviate this problem. But the grants came over the course of the year and ended up being spent on numerous other necessities—notably food—so that by the time the school year came around, few families had money for the fees. African Medical Mission budgeted to cover these fees, and it was Mkuseli's job to figure out how this money was to be apportioned to cover the more than one hundred students who needed help. Many children made do with hand-me-down uniforms, but these were often so frayed and ratty that in addition to paying fees, AMM—Mkuseli—purchased a small number of shirts, shoes, trousers, and skirts.

Eager to learn more about education, I accompanied Mkuseli on his rounds in the first week of school. Our first stop was the school itself. Mkuseli and I sat in the school office, and he and a teacher went through the list of each student AMM was paying fees for. I didn't last long. I couldn't stand watching the school official handwrite—with agonizing slowness, interrupted for conversation every now and again—118 receipts. Mkuseli was more than capable of handling the situation himself so I wandered outside to explore what we were paying for.

The school was formally known as the Itipini Junior Secondary School, but everyone referred to it as Ezra after the name of the first principal. The school had been built in 1994, in the midst of the excitement and energy that surrounded the transition to democracy and the reintegration of the Transkei into South Africa. Ezra was long gone but stories about him still circulated. He had been a firm disciplinarian but the school had functioned more or less as a school should.

That was then. Now, as I strolled the grounds, I found what I had come to expect in the Transkei. Two long brick buildings surrounded a yard mostly of dirt and rocks. Many of the windows in the classrooms were broken. Where there was grass, it was tall and weedy. The classrooms were overcrowded and there weren't enough desks and chairs to go around. Many students sat on the bare concrete floor or on a mixed collection of mostly broken plastic chairs. The room set aside as a library had a few old computers no one knew how to work and a ragged collection of books. There weren't any bathrooms, and the only water in the whole school was a faucet at the far end of the compound. There were better schools in Mthatha, I knew, much better. I thought about how much I wanted each preschool student I had seen graduate the year before to attend one of those schools, where they would have, at the least, a chair to sit in and books to read. But Ezra was what was nearby and what the families—and AMM—could realistically afford.

Later that week, Mkuseli and I went shopping for clothes. Given his height, he could have easily vanished in the aisles that were crowded with school uniform shoppers. But with his notebook and pen firmly in hand, he held forth in a commanding style, directing a small army of store employees this way and that. I had encouraged him to list each item and the number he needed of each size. For instance, six pairs of size eight shoes or five pairs of size ten shoes. That message hadn't gotten through. Instead, he went through his list in the order he had made it, that is, in the random and haphazard order in which mothers had approached him. "Shoes, size six! Shoes, size eight! Trousers, size ten!" he called out, and a pile of clothing gradually grew up in front of him. I sighed. This was how things worked in Mthatha and it was another job Mkuseli could handle himself. I bought a newspaper and waited outside.

Mkuseli was eager to have me meet his family and show me his home. We had a little time on the way back from one of our trips into town and he insisted on making a detour into Ngangalizwe, the large and sprawling township on the outside of town, just up the hill behind Itipini. He pointed me to a row of cinder block houses on the side of the road and I pulled over.

I hadn't given much thought to Mkuseli's home life before this trip and didn't know what to expect. What he had, though, stunned me. It was a small room, probably ten feet by ten feet. He shared the space with his wife, Nosibabalo, and their six-year-old daughter, Lelethu. There was a small refrigerator and a two-burner hot plate in one corner; that was the kitchen. Near the door was a small bench, facing a set of shelves; that was the living room. On the other side of the shelves was a bed. At least that's what I surmised. That morning, there was so little room to move around I couldn't maneuver my way past Mkuseli, by the kitchen, and around the shelves to see what was on the other side. I took a seat on the rickety bench.

I was struggling to process the fact that my bathroom was almost as big as the entire room but Mkuseli took an inordinate amount of pride in pointing out each feature of his home. There was the television with grainy reception and CD player that were the focal point of the living room. There were the faux china figurines and plaques of inspirational sayings that dotted the wall. The water tap was right outside so Nosibabalo didn't have to go far to cook and clean. The toilet was down the alley and shared by all the residents of the similar rooms nearby. His home was, indeed, his castle. He dug around for some carrots and insisted that we have a snack before returning to work.

Mkuseli lived a step or two higher on the socioeconomic ladder than did people in Itipini—his house was made of cinder block, after all, not scrap metal—and he became my window into the life of those who were poor, but not abjectly so. Twenty years earlier, he had finished his high school diploma in a rural Transkei village and come to Mthatha looking for work. He hadn't had any luck so, like many other young men from the rural Transkei before him, he set out to the mines near Johannesburg that were the backbone of the South African economy. But it was the late 1980s, the mines were drying up and, along with it, the need for manual labor from the large unskilled black population in South Africa. There was little need for a short and slight young man.

He had returned to the Transkei, floating between his rural home and Mthatha for some time before landing a job as a guard with a local security company. The only place in Mthatha he could find to stay was in a community on the far outskirts of town. It was a shantytown similar to Itipini, with the notable distinction that it was not built on a landfill. He walked into town every day for work, several kilometers each way, because he couldn't afford the taxi fare. Meanwhile, he was trying to figure out a way to marry Nosibabalo. In order to do so, he needed to round up several cows, or their worth in rand, to pay her family the *lobola* or bride price. But he wasn't being paid enough to live on, let alone save for a wedding. She stayed in their rural village home.

A decade before I arrived in Itipini, Jenny hired him to coordinate after-school activities. His income increased, which allowed him to move to Ngangalizwe to be closer to Itipini and to save money and marry Nosibabalo. He had a much shorter commute, a wife, and, soon, a daughter. By the time I arrived, he was well established in his home, Lelethu was about to start school, he was a trusted staff member at Itipini, and he even had the money to take his family back to their rural village once a month or so to visit his mother.

But many challenges remained. Nosibabalo, a large, welcoming woman who also had a high school diploma, couldn't find work. She was taking correspondence classes to become a social worker, but it was only part-time because she had a family to look after and it would be a long time before she finished the degree. Even if she did, there was no guarantee there would be work once she had.

The visit to his home was one more step in the deepening of our relationship, and Mkuseli began to go out of his way to invite me into his life. I joined him one weekend at his rural home for a family gathering centered on the unveiling of the tombstone for his grandmother and some other relatives. Amid the vast open expanses of the rural Transkei and the colorful mud-brick huts, we prayed over the tombstones and ate a giant meal cooked by a small army of women in cast-iron cauldrons over open flames. Some time later, when Nosibabalo gave birth to a second daughter, Mkuseli insisted that I come up to meet Kungawo the day after the birth. Sitting on their bed and cradling her in my arms, I wondered how the family would fit a fourth body into their small home.

I was working longer and longer days in Itipini as my responsibilities accumulated, which meant I began to see Mkuseli at work in the afternoon. If my respect and appreciation for him deepened the more I came to know of his family, it went the other way the more I saw of him at work.

The AMM office had been given a large pile of books and I was eager to put them to use in some sort of library. As I envisioned it, the project would be for the benefit of the children in the after-school program. This was Mkuseli's turf so I sat down with him one morning to explain in general terms about the books and how we might make them available to the children. His eyes lit up: "A library!" he said excitedly. I was relieved. He had mentioned the idea of a library before I had. Surely that was a good sign—he supported the project and would help make it a reality. We decided the best place would be the back half of the shipping container he used as his office. I brought in a bookshelf, a visiting group of volunteers painted the walls, and we laid down some carpet squares. We seemed set.

The trouble was I hadn't pursued the initial conversation with Mkuseli far enough. Once he bought into the idea of a library, it never occurred to me to discuss the how or the who: how would it function, who would be responsible. I knew what a library was like; I assumed he did too.

But it turned out that Mkuseli didn't like having a lot of children in "his" shipping container. When a group of preschool children came in after lunch and asked to color, I would delightedly set them up on the tables and chairs I had arranged. It was exactly what I had hoped for. Seeing them coloring productively, I would step out to attend to business elsewhere. When I returned, even if I had been gone only a few minutes, they had vanished. I sought them out again and encouraged them to come back. When I saw them coloring productively again, I slipped out and returned to the clinic. Again, when I came back to the library, they had vanished. This time when I asked them to return they shook their heads. "No, he'll yell at us." I realized what was happening. The library wasn't Mkuseli's project; it wasn't even "our" project. It was my idea, and if I wasn't around to supervise the children and lay claim to the space and time, he wanted the area for himself. But I had other responsibilities. That's why I had wanted Mkuseli involved from the beginning. The library limped along, dependent on my presence for its success.

The after-school program was responsible for a large plot of land that had been set aside for a garden. It was a good idea. The students learned about gardening, tended it regularly, and made money by selling the produce. The soil—helped along by the generations of pigs who had trod Itipini—was rich and fertile. The corn grew like bamboo during the summer, the beetroot was larger than my fist, and the spinach leaves were longer than my arm. Jenny and I oohed and ahhed appreciatively at the produce and stocked up on vegetables.

But it wasn't quite what I imagined the garden to be. When it was time to plant, Mkuseli rounded up a collection of students to help him out. Most of the time, though, I saw him weeding and watering in the morning when the students were still in school. Mkuseli clearly measured the success of the garden by the size and quantity of the produce. But that missed the point. The purpose of the garden was to give the students responsibility for a project of their own, teach them about agriculture, and keep them busy after school. I cared less about the garden's produce than I did about how much the children were learning. Under Mkuseli's tutelage, I wasn't sure they were learning much.

The garden was indicative of a larger problem: Mkuseli had little or no rapport with the students who were supposed to be his charge. I had begun working with a small group of students after school and at one session I asked Mkuseli to translate a few crucial bits of information. I wanted the students to know that I would stay after school to help them with homework and that they were welcome to attend these sessions. I said this in a gentle and conversational tone. It was an invitation to an optional class.

Mkuseli turned to the students and drew himself up to his full height. He let loose a stream of Xhosa at full volume and pitch. I could tell from the start he wasn't just translating my words. He was adding his own "polish" to them. I didn't catch much of what he said, but when he finished he turned to me with a satisfied smile on his face.

"What did you say?" I asked.

"I told them if they don't come to your class, they will not get any snack for the rest of the year and won't be able to go to the clinic."

I was appalled. It went against everything I knew about working with young adults. Mkuseli had made threats he either couldn't or wouldn't enforce. He had no input on the clinic, and he delegated snack distribution to some of the students who would not know to prevent my students from getting snack. But I swallowed, smiled, and thanked him. Then I turned to the students and in the mildest tone I could muster said, "See you Friday." Fortunately, they returned, and I resolved to minimize Mkuseli's future involvement with this particular group of students.

Driving away from Itipini that afternoon, I ruefully thought about what Mkuseli had said to the students. "Doesn't he understand anything about leadership?" I thought. "Doesn't he understand how to be a servant and the importance of building relationships with the students?" It was like a light bulb had gone off. The questions answered themselves. Of course he didn't know about these things. The ideas about leadership I was using to judge him were shaped by the cultural environment in which I was raised and the many people I knew over the years who modeled what it meant to be a servant leader. Mkuseli had none of this.

Our differing backgrounds meant Mkuseli and I were approaching our jobs from two wildly different perspectives. I wanted the children to be able to learn and grow, regardless of what the output of the garden was. I wanted our interactions to be rooted in deep relationships. I wanted to put the children's needs first and build programs around them. I knew that the only way students would respond to me is if they first knew me and could trust me. In many years of summer camp counseling, I had learned about developing a rapport with children that delineated the boundaries of acceptable action but also encouraged a sense of playfulness within those boundaries. Successful discipline strategies flowed from preexisting relationships with children and avoided raised voices. Mkuseli, obviously, had never had any of this kind of experience. He knew he was supposed to be in charge of the students, and he expected them to follow his direction. I saw little emphasis on relationship building in his work. He had the title and position of after-school director, and he expected everyone to listen to him as a result.

The trouble was people didn't usually listen to him. When he was the MC for a public event like the preschool graduation or a World AIDS Day celebration and told people to be quiet, they ignored him and kept on talking. When he called choir rehearsals and few of his singers showed up, he blamed the students for their absence, not thinking that if he spent time getting to know them better they might be more willing to show up for his rehearsals. The result was that Mkuseli was less effective in his position than I wished he could have been. He would not have lasted long as program director at any summer camp I knew.

But how effective could he have been? Our different approaches came not just from our different backgrounds but from our different cultures as well. In Xhosa culture, the needs of children barely count. I attended countless funerals and family gatherings in which men were served food first, then women, and then children. Why would I expect Mkuseli to do any differently? He had struggled and scraped by in school without much help. When he saw young people struggling with school, he didn't see a child in need of help, he saw a child experiencing exactly what he had experienced and what was simply normal. Moreover, his was a much more tenuous existence than mine. If the produce in the garden could offset a portion of his—and others'—grocery bills, that was money that could be spent on other pressing needs. There was little patience for the idea that the process of learning mattered more than the product of the garden.

I was seeing Itipini through the lens of my own values and experience. I believed in putting the needs of others ahead of my own as a form of service. I believed I could reject the authority I had by virtue of my position as a rich, white male and establish a new source of authority based on the relationships I built. If I was going to save anyone, this is how it was going to happen, and it motivated my incarnational approach in Itipini. But even this basic approach was a luxury that only someone in my position could afford. Part of being incarnational, I realized, was that my efforts were mediated through the preexisting staff and network of relationships into which I entered when I decided to work in Itipini. Mkuseli became and remained one of my closest friends in Itipini and taught me much about his culture and way of life. I struggled to teach him more about mine.

Six

Charlie's Angels

THE PURCHASE OF A pair of socks does not generally mark a turning point in many lives. But on a sweltering January afternoon, standing in the aisle of one of many stores in Mthatha selling school uniforms, I purchased ten pairs of socks and realized that my time in Itipini was continuing to change.

I was with five high school students—all female—who had finished grade nine the previous year and asked African Medical Mission for financial support to make the transition to grade ten and high school. On this Friday afternoon, we were shopping for the clothes they needed for the new uniforms required at Nozuko High School. They all still wore the uniforms from their old schools, which showed every indication that they had been worn every single day for the previous year. The shirts were frayed and ripped at the collars, the sweaters had holes in them, and the soles were coming loose from the shoes. But it was the socks that grabbed my attention. They were full of holes and worn thin. I thought about all the pairs of socks I had sweated through and worn out working in Itipini the previous few months. These young women had worn the exact same pair of socks, five days a week, for the entire year. I looked at the price tag. It was about eighty cents a pair. I looked again at the feet of the students, milling around in the aisles, trying on new shoes and searching for the right sized shirt.

"Okay," I said. "Everyone can get two pairs of socks."

Five surprised faces turned to look at me. Immediately, they gathered around the sock section and began a complicated decision-making process. If they could have two pairs of socks, did they want two of the same style? Or should one be ankle socks and another knee-length? There were also a few pairs of socks that came to mid-calf. How did these affect the calculations? I stepped back, content to let them make their own decisions.

When these young women had shown up asking for help a week or so earlier, I volunteered to take on the task of getting them into school. Mkuseli was busy with the primary students, and I was eager to expand my role in Itipini and learn something new about education. The students were new to high school and I was new to the beginning of a school year in Mthatha. Blindly, we stepped forward together.

Our first chunk of time together had come on a rainy Thursday morning. Because of the high crime rate, the school refused to accept payment of fees any other way but by direct deposit into their bank account. Given the complexities of sorting through receipts and bank statements from hundreds of students, essentially the entire first week of school was given over to registration and organization. The five young women had come to show me the paperwork from school to prove they had been registered. In return, I was going to give them the bank receipts that showed we had paid the school fees. Predictably, everything had not gone precisely as planned. Their registration paperwork wasn't quite filled out because they didn't have the necessary ID photos to attach to their forms. They seemed to think I could produce those with my camera. I couldn't, but I had an idea.

Outside the Department of Home Affairs, several women make their living by taking Polaroid ID photos so people who are applying for government identity documents can get them on the spot. I had encountered them on the multiple trips I made in search of a permanent visa in my first weeks in Mthatha. I suggested the students head there for the picture. Onele, whose English was the best of the five, pointed at the sky. "It's raining," she said. "We need to be in school. Can't you give us a ride?" It was a quiet clinic day—it always was when it rained—so I borrowed the *bakkie* and we set off down the muddy road.

We must have been quite the sight when we got out of the car in town, five short young women in fraying school uniforms and one tall white man in shorts and a T-shirt. As I crossed the street to find a photographer, Onele told me I stood out for another reason: "You hurry everywhere!" (In the Transkei, moving at anything faster than an amble is not common practice.) We found a woman who could do the pictures, and the Polaroids developed quickly.

As we got back in the car, I sensed a new problem had arisen but it took me a minute to grasp it in our fractured English/Xhosa dialogue. The pictures needed to be attached to the application and they needed a stapler to do that. Apparently, they couldn't count on finding one at school. Very soon this rose to the level of a serious problem. We happened to be stuck in the middle of downtown Mthatha traffic, close to an Internet café I frequented. I pulled in, gave my best smile, borrowed the stapler, and ran back outside, dodging raindrops. "You hurry everywhere," I heard again. Soon enough, we were on the road again.

As we drove away, I realized I had only the vaguest idea of where the school was. All five students knew, but each had a different way of getting there, and each insisted on giving directions—in Xhosa—simultaneously. Dodging traffic and pedestrians, I gamely tried to listen but it was no use. We took several wrong turns before I asked Onele to explain in her best English just how to get to the school. The classrooms were jammed full of students trying to register when we finally arrived. My five only added to the crush when they got out. Everything was now in order with their applications. The school year had begun.

*

Mkuseli had spoken with the mothers of the primary students about what uniform parts their children needed for school. That was fine for him, but I had no desire to personally interview five adolescent women about clothing and clothing sizes. Much easier and safer, I thought, to take them along on a shopping trip and let them pick out what they needed. Plus, it would be a good opportunity to see town through their eyes. A week after their registrations were accepted, we set off.

The troubles quickly mounted, however. All five had made do throughout their school careers with hand-me-downs and whatever else their families could scrounge together. But they were the first in their families to make it to high school so there were no hand-me-downs to be had. As a result, the experience of buying new clothes directly off the rack with the tags still on was overwhelming. Their response to the novelty of the situation was mostly commendable: each made careful and deliberate decisions. To me, each pair of trousers looked the same. But to them there were subtle and profound differences, which meant we had to traipse to store after store looking for just the right pair. It took ages.

When they weren't deliberating over identical pairs of trousers, the five students were quick to confuse needs with wants. Our common vocabulary was relatively limited but I could still tell when a student's eye lighted on something new. She would turn to me and begin to make a convincing case in mixed Xhosa and English as to why it was just the item she needed for this school year. I was ignorant of what was really required at school but I also had a tight budget and didn't want to begin the year on a buying spree that could set the tone for the remainder of our relationship. I spent the afternoon trying to strike a balance—yes to the extra pair of socks, for instance, but no to the colored pencils—failing more often than I succeeded.

The combined effect of the afternoon was that within just a few minutes I realized my students were confirming every single stereotype of women and shopping I had ever known: it took forever to make a decision and they wanted everything they set their eyes on. As I trailed along, I felt like nothing so much as a harried father glumly following his daughters around, money in hand. In my thinking about mission and helping people in Itipini, I had not expected to be reduced to the role of ATM, dispensing money as needed. But if they showed up on Monday in their old uniforms, their teachers would send them home. This was something I could do and it was necessary.

By the time the stores began to close for the day, we were hot and tired and I sat us down for an ice cream cone in the fading heat. The students stared at their cones, holding them awkwardly in their hands as the ice cream melted quickly. It dawned on me they didn't know what to do. A few were making uncertain attempts on their own. Unsure of the appropriate Xhosa vocabulary—or even how I would begin to teach someone to eat an ice cream cone in English—I set into mine, hoping the example would suffice. It did. They leaned into their cones, tentatively at first but learning rapidly from their experience. The ice cream was soon gone, a satisfying end to an exhausting afternoon at the end of a long week.

℮↝

Anne, my YASC predecessor in Itipini, had dedicated a significant amount of time to a Bible study that many of the young mothers attended regularly. When I had met Anne briefly, she asked me to continue this group and I agreed to do my best, though I was skeptical what insight a white, childless male who didn't speak any Xhosa could bring to her group. I was too new and couldn't replicate her rapport with them. In my first few months, the group had slowly disbanded. But these students presented an opportunity and I didn't want to lose it. This was my moment to begin—at last—to make a contribution to Itipini. English-language skill was critical to these students' future work prospects. As my early interactions demonstrated, their English was rudimentary at best. I could create a similar group to Anne's and work on teaching them English.

Teaching English is perhaps the stereotypical overseas assignment for young, eager Americans looking to make a difference in the world. This can be a powerful and important use of young Americans' time but as I was considering options for overseas work, teaching English held little appeal. I feared that teaching English to nonnative speakers would be akin to my experience teaching swimming to nonswimmers. Swimming had come easily to me but I struggled to teach basic swimming techniques to others. Most of the time I found myself wanting to yell, "You just get in the water and swim! How hard is that?" My experience with the ice cream cones notwithstanding, I was, perhaps, not a natural teacher and began our group in Itipini with suitably low expectations.

But I could relate to the position my students were in. When I arrived in Itipini, the initial hurdle I needed to overcome in speaking Xhosa was my pride and my fear of making mistakes in front of others. Once I realized how welcoming and forgiving people in Itipini were of my efforts, however, I was able to try new words and grammatical constructions without damaging my pride too much. My English students had a similar reluctance to try to speak a new language and risk embarrassment in front of their friends. They had a tenuous grasp of some basic words and concepts and, with some struggle, could read English text. But they never had any reinforcement at home, never needed English in their daily life, and lacked the confidence necessary to practice their English and so improve it. The major block they had to improving their language was, in part, knowledge of the language, but mainly comfort and security in that knowledge. What they needed was a comfortable environment in which to practice and make mistakes.

Those first, frustrating few months in Itipini proved to be an excellent, if unintentional, foundation for the English class. I had crossed paths in the clinic with all the students at some point. One, Victoria, had been critical in helping me care for a patient with AIDS in the last days of her life and accompanied me on numerous trips to the hospital. Three of the students were mothers and I knew their children from baby clinic days. When I had done nothing in those first few months except smile at people and play with children, I was actually putting myself into the community and making myself a known quantity. The emphasis I placed on sharing an existence with people in Itipini and simply being—no matter how frustrating it was—meant I already knew the students and the students knew of me. Those relationships, I hoped, would create an environment in which they could try out new words and safely make mistakes.

But relationships only go so far; preparation and organization help. I was poorly prepared for the first few meetings and they sputtered into lifeless squibs before they even started, making me wonder again what particular gifts I brought to teaching in these circumstances. We laughed and maybe learned a little bit together but it wasn't a sustainable model. Mostly, I found myself overwhelmed by the contrast. I was the college-educated, single, well-fed white man whose only housing complaint was that my roof leaked a bit when it rained. They were a group of young women, all too old for their grades, some mothers already, few of whom could point out South Africa on a map, none of whom lived in homes with electricity or running water or routinely had enough to eat. At one early meeting, the biggest disagreement was over who should get the extra apples I brought along.

Grasping for structure, I found my inspiration in a teacher friend of mine who led an after-school book club for her second-grade students. Armed with several copies of Roald Dahl's *Charlie and the Chocolate Factory*, I had my syllabus for the next few months: read the book, out loud, two days a week. Reading out loud would give these young women a chance to work on their pronunciation and build a comfort level with new and difficult words. It would provide an easy opening for reading comprehension questions. Reading the same book would provide the necessary incentive to keep these students returning to what was, after all, only an optional meeting. I picked *Charlie* because that was what my friend was reading in South Carolina. I didn't know much about assessing reading levels; I blindly guessed that a group of second-grade private school students in South Carolina would be at about the same reading level as my students, ten to twelve years and a lifetime of experiences older.

The results were mixed. There were all the usual group-related challenges of varying skill levels and levels of interest, not to mention the fear of embarrassment in front of one's friends. Navigating these in another language was, like everything else, aggravating. I stopped frequently to test their comprehension and the students gave me confused looks and seemed unable to answer some pretty basic questions. I had forgotten how frequently Dahl resorts to made-up words. Too many of those in a row would have the students complaining about how difficult it was.

The life of Charlie Bucket, the protagonist, is not, in the early chapters, all that different from life in Itipini. Indeed, it is probably marginally more dire. He lives in a run-down home outside town with his extended family, is desperately poor, and is close to starvation. For the first few chapters, several students thought they were reading a work of nonfiction. When we got to the chapter on the building of a chocolate palace, I wasn't sure if the puzzled looks on their faces were a good or a bad sign.

But learning was, indeed, occurring, no matter that it came in fits and starts. We sat on plastic chairs and benches in the converted shipping container that had once been the clinic. Without electricity, it was dark in the container so we had to leave the big door open. This cut both ways. It let in the noise of the younger children on the playground but it also allowed the students who were mothers to keep an eye on their children who toddled around just outside. More skilled students started helping those who struggled. They sounded out words together and tried to comprehend difficult passages. When we reached the end of a chapter and concluded our sessions, I thought I detected a few looks of modest disappointment.

Around lunchtime one Wednesday some months into the school year, Lindiwe came to find me. It wasn't surprising that she wasn't in school during the middle of the day. School occasionally and randomly ended early. More often, the students skipped, complaining of mysterious colds or "fevers," a catch-all term that could refer to almost any ailment. If they weren't sick, they had numerous responsibilities at home that kept them busy. Lindiwe had a young son and often that meant she missed at least a day of school each week. On this day, I asked with resignation why she wasn't in school, expecting a familiar answer.

"I need help on my homework," she replied. This was surprising. I frequently told the students that I was available to help them with their homework but they rarely took me up on the offer. Usually they had to get home to the chores they knew awaited them after our reading group. But if they wanted help, they were supposed to find me after school, not in the middle of the day. Lindiwe had already missed the bulk of the day, however, so I asked her to show me the assignment. It was a document-based assignment, familiar to me from my high school courses. The student was given a series of short readings from historical sources and, based on those readings and the student's own knowledge, had to answer a series of questions about the assigned topic. Lindiwe's topic, clearly written across the first page, was "16th Century West African Empires."

"When is this due?" I asked, racking my brain for the slightest bit of knowledge about sixteenth-century empires of any kind.

"Tomorrow," she said. That explained why she hadn't waited to see me after school. I thought about mentioning something to her about how much more helpful I could have been if she had approached me when the project had been assigned. But it was too late for that.

We sat down in the shipping container and began to look at the assignment. I rapidly realized that not only did Lindiwe seem to know less about sixteenth-century West African empires than I did, she didn't even comprehend the assignment. We looked at the assignment as a whole. What was she being asked to do? How did the documents relate to the questions? What were the documents for? It was no good. She had a tightly constrained view of what she needed to do—write down an answer for each question so she could have something to hand in the next day. Given the late hour, I couldn't blame her.

I asked her to read me the first question. She struggled through it. I asked her which documents would help her answer it. There was a confused look on her face. I realized we had skipped a step. I asked her to look at the documents and tell me what they were about. She began reading aloud the first one. It was a struggle. The words were right but there was not even a glimmer of comprehension on her face. It was going to be a long session.

The assignment was a major part of Lindiwe's grade for that marking period. But she didn't understand the questions. She didn't understand the documents she was supposed to use to answer the questions. The whole concept of West African empires was foreign to her. There was no preexisting knowledge to draw on, though I couldn't tell if this was because Lindiwe missed the days of class when they covered the subject or if it was just never covered. At this point, who was to blame mattered little.

We struggled through the assignment. I attempted to simplify the English in the documents so she understood them. When I could, I translated some phrases into my rudimentary Xhosa. There were a few occasional and brief glimmers of comprehension on her face but they quickly passed. She kept looking at me expectantly, as if I would tell her exactly what to write down in response to each question. I didn't do that but I came close, pointing her to the relevant portion of each document. She would give an "Ah!" as if she understood what was going on but it was clear she didn't. She was just humoring me to keep me going. In the end, with the help of a visiting volunteer, we got something down for most of the questions but it hadn't been a constructive learning experience for Lindiwe. She wasn't walking away with any new knowledge.

Not much later, two other students asked for help on a project about the sources of electricity in South Africa. The first few questions asked about how oil, natural gas, and nuclear fuel could be used to generate electricity. I had recently stumbled across a small public library in the Ngangalizwe township near Itipini and offered to take them there. We flipped through an old World Book Encyclopedia from 1992, the exact same edition I had consulted for assignments in elementary school. They dutifully found the section on nuclear fuel and began copying it word for word into their notebooks. It was clear they didn't understand a word of what they were writing down—it was written in English, after all, for native English speakers—but it qualified as completing the assignment. By having something to hand in, they would no doubt be a step ahead of some of their classmates.

It was the final part of the assignment that most confused them. They were asked to consider ways they used electricity in their own home and how they could conserve it. It was a fine question to ask of any student and it might have encouraged some reflection on personal energy consumption. It overlooked the minor matter that these students lived in shacks on a former garbage dump without running water or electricity. How did the teacher expect them to answer that question?

The resources the students were given weren't always helpful. One student's history textbook was a brand-new tome about African history after decolonization, several hundred pages long, published in the same year she was using it by a premier European academic publisher I recognized. Part of me was a little jealous at what they were covering in class, and I wanted to borrow the book to fill in some of the gaps left by my American education. But for the student it was mostly incomprehensible. It was entirely in English—the sort of English that a premier academic publisher would use in a textbook. This student was being given the resources she needed to succeed in this class but for her to even make it through one page of the textbook and understand it took far too long.

The more I learned about just how steep were the challenges these students faced in school, the more *Charlie and the Chocolate Factory* seemed pretty insignificant.

✒

Nonetheless, the initial group of five students soon grew. Word got around their social circles that there was an English class in Itipini. Given the dearth of after-school opportunities in Mthatha—and the free fruit I handed out at the end of class—a few new faces started showing up. A handful became regular members of the group so that within a few months of meeting, my group was up to nine members. A few months of class were too little to tell if my efforts were having any discernible impact on the grades of these students. It was too soon to tell if my interest in their education would make them any more regular in their attendance or try any harder at their work. But those first few months had a tremendous impact on my attitude about what I could do in Itipini.

I never forced the students to come. There were no consequences if they missed a class. If they missed a few in a row, I would go check on them to make sure nothing was wrong and that they were still going to school. Often they were; they just had to miss a class because there were too many chores to do once they returned from school to be able to fit in my class. I had nothing tangible to offer them beyond a snack and a friendly smile. And yet they continued to come. More than that, they even seemed to enjoy reading about Charlie Bucket and Willy Wonka.

I found myself wishing we had enough vocabulary in common so that I could tell them how much their attendance and largely positive attitudes meant to me. I had been searching throughout my first months in Itipini for a way to actually *do* something, to make a positive and substantive contribution to the community. In meeting with these students a few days a week after school, I finally began to feel like I was doing exactly that. The mere fact of their attendance began to validate the long-ago thought that I should move to Africa to "save" Africans. I was most assuredly not saving anyone. But I was finally beginning to enjoy myself, to see myself and be seen as a small part of the complicated texture of life in Itipini. The frustrations of cultural and language barriers were still there—they were a constant—but now they were tinged with a slight hue of modest accomplishment. Now when I found myself frustrated, I could fall back on comforting thoughts of success about what my time in Itipini had amounted to. And slowly, without perhaps realizing it at first, I knew I might need more than a single year in Itipini.

Seven

Live and Learn?

ASIDE FROM MKUSELI, THERE were a dozen or so other staff in Itipini. They were a long-tenured lot. The women in the kitchen had been working there from the time Jenny had decided to add a lunch program for the children. They had witnessed the evolution of the cooking facilities from an iron cauldron over an open fire to stainless steel pots on a propane range. The head teacher in the preschool, Ncediwe, had been around so long that some of her former students had already become mothers themselves and had children ready for preschool.

At the heart of the staff, when I arrived, was Thandeka. She was as long-tenured as anyone else and in charge of the daily distribution of cornmeal and bread to the HIV patients. She ran it efficiently and with a smile on her face. By the time we arrived each morning, she had already arranged the bags of cornmeal and set up the table and bucket from which she would distribute. Immediately after our prayers, as the line of patients formed around her, the first of the bags went into her bucket and she began her routine, smoothly scooping the cornmeal into each outstretched container. She had the list of patients in her head. She knew who should get what and she knew who sometimes collected on behalf of someone else. The only interruption to her routine was to empty another bag of cornmeal into her bucket. In just a few minutes, she was done, and moved quickly to the loaves of bread. The routine there was the same. Not long after that, with the patients satisfied and wandering back to their shacks, she had a broom in her hand, sweeping up the detritus and making sure there was enough food for the next day. On Fridays, when we distributed more food and other items to patients, she was equally efficient, pivoting from sugar to beans to soap.

Thandeka's daily routine—along with the activities of the preschool children—provided a constant and steadying rhythm that pulsed through the morning hours at the clinic. In those early weeks and months I may not have known what to do but at least, I thought, Thandeka did. The thought was a comforting one but it was tinged with intimidation, that everything ran so smoothly, and a little jealousy, that Thandeka should have such a well-defined place in the community while I struggled to figure out what mine was.

Sometimes we crossed paths in the kitchen. She took her breaks there, as I did, and checked on her two young grandchildren. They were cousins, the daughter and son of Thandeka's two oldest daughters. The daughters were in high school at the time so Thandeka provided most of the care during the day. The energy in the kitchen spun around and centered on her, and the other staff clearly looked to her as a leader and a mentor. Because she only spoke Xhosa and I was still new, our interactions were limited and brief.

Aside from her two daughters, Thandeka had a younger son and a third daughter. She lived with them, her grandchildren, and her husband, who worked for the municipality. His name was Richard, and it was hard to see what task of value he could perform for any employer. He frequently came to the clinic complaining of various ailments, all of which seemed to be related to the overconsumption of alcohol. He made sure never to leave without the sick note we could write to excuse him from work.

On Fridays, our goal was to have an education session after the morning prayers, trying to share some nugget of wisdom that might lead to a small change in behavior: the importance of personal hygiene, for instance, or immunizing children on schedule. One Friday, Thandeka gave an impressively energetic performance of a song that had her dancing around our little meeting area. The only word I caught was "condoms" and only because it was repeated so frequently and with such gusto. Hearing her sing about sex so openly only deepened my appreciation for her, especially since so many other people in Itipini preferred to ignore the subject altogether.

But when we drove into Itipini one morning, we didn't see Thandeka in her usual routine. Another staff member was filling in, which wasn't unusual. Occasionally, staff members got sick or had to take care of business in town and they planned ahead and arranged coverage among themselves. But this was more serious. The previous night Thandeka had been transferring a cooking pot off the fire and in so doing had spilled boiling water over her chest and arm and suffered significant burns. When Jenny went to visit her in the hospital, it was clear she needed a prolonged stay. But Thandeka didn't like the hospital and wasn't satisfied with her treatment. They didn't change her dressings often enough, she said, and didn't treat her well. About a week after the accident, she checked herself out in frustration and returned to Itipini.

It was a shadow of her previous self that walked back through the clinic doors. She had lost weight and moved slowly and gingerly. Her arm and chest were swathed in bandages, and changing the dressings took ages, first to gently unwrap them, then clean the wounds and apply new dressings. She must have been in terrible pain but she smiled and did a little dance step when we asked how she was feeling. When I offered to give her a ride down the road to be closer to her shack, she refused and limped along herself. Given the hygiene issues caused by living on a dump, it was miraculous that her wounds didn't get immediately infected at home.

Caring for Thandeka put a tremendous burden on the clinic. Jenny pleaded with her to return to the hospital to get the care she needed. Thandeka flatly refused. But worried, perhaps, that Jenny would drag her back to the hospital and force her to be readmitted, she spent only a few days in Itipini before returning to her rural village. Her daughters told us that she was being treated there. But that was no relief. No understaffed and ill-stocked rural clinic could give her the care she needed.

She returned after a few weeks, her wounds slathered in red floor polish, the home remedy she had opted for in the village. She looked even worse than when she first left the hospital, clearly dehydrated, even thinner, and very worn. When we arrived in Itipini two days later, the first thing we were told was that she had died the night before. Devastation was written clearly across the faces of a distraught staff. Though I knew Thandeka less well than they, I shared in their loss as I realized how comforting it had been to see Thandeka work so professionally and competently every morning.

Thandeka had been not only the pivot point of the staff but the glue holding her family together. Shortly after her death, her children and husband descended into a soap operatic nightmare that was tragic for all concerned. Richard was given a spousal death benefit by the municipality and promptly began living with another woman, rarely showing his face in the clinic again. The older daughters and their younger brother fought about everything and occasionally appeared in the clinic sporting a new black eye or cut lip. It was impossible to know how to help or even if intervention would make any difference. The sisters stopped going to school and started jointly caring for their children and their younger sister. Thandeka's son gradually drifted out of Itipini altogether.

I was mostly an observer of Thandeka's care. She knew Jenny best and there was little I could have contributed that Jenny couldn't do herself. I shared the sense of tragedy the staff felt when Thandeka died. It was a privilege to join with them in the darkness of Thandeka's shack the afternoon she died and to listen as they sang and prayed their grief. A few days later, the entire community crowded into the after-school gym for a memorial service that remembered Thandeka's daily work for the community. It was difficult to see someone die a preventable death, but I convinced myself that my own feelings of ineffectuality in watching Thandeka die were a temporary phase, one I could move beyond when I gained more experience. I was kidding myself.

A few weeks after Thandeka's death, on a typically frustrating day in the clinic, I stepped outside for a break. I had managed to find a few cards, dispense a few medications, and bandage a wound or two, but I kept returning to the feelings of uselessness and incomprehension that had bedeviled me since I arrived. As I sat down on the bench outside the clinic some older primary students walked by, out of school early and on their way home. I knew several of them and, to my delight, they stopped to talk to me. It wasn't entirely in Xhosa nor entirely in English but in some fractured combination of the two. We relied heavily on body language and tone of voice to make ourselves understood. But we were actually exchanging moderately complex thoughts. The language barrier was crumbling further.

I asked what they were learning in school and they showed me a Xhosa-language play they were reading. I entertained by attempting to read it, provoking laughter at my inability to pronounce any word longer than a syllable or two. In return, they wanted to know when and where I had gone to school. As we sat there I could have almost forgotten I was sitting in a shantytown in South Africa; it just seemed like I was hanging out with friends, which, I realized, I was.

An insistent woman interrupted us, motioning me to come inside the clinic so she could get her husband's daily tuberculosis pills. But I was busy declaiming Xhosa poetry so I pointed out a visiting volunteer in the clinic who could help her. She stared right at me and said, emphatically, "ndifuna wena"—"I want you." I had understood what she meant immediately. That alone was glorious, further evidence that day that I was beginning to surmount the language barrier. That she truly meant it affirmed for me that I was wanted—my deep desire!—by at least one person in Itipini. True, she only needed me to dispense four pills and make a tick mark on a chart. But it was something. I got up and got the pills.

Progress kept coming. It came in small increments, measured by two-word phrases, but it was coming nonetheless.

The woman's name was, oddly, NoFirst, and she was in her early thirties. She lived with her family in a large and sprawling shack on the hill directly above the clinic. The front room was a small spaza shop—a convenience store—from which she sold necessities like paraffin, fruit, cornmeal, and sugar for people unable or unwilling to make it into town to purchase their own goods. The shop also doubled as a *shebeen*, and I frequently heard loud music pulsating from the hill above and saw many drunk customers sitting in the sun in front of the door, slowly passing around an old five-liter paint can full of homebrew.

Both NoFirst and her husband Lindumzi were, like many other couples in Itipini, HIV positive. Lindumzi had TB when I arrived and NoFirst herself had been through TB treatment about two years earlier. In my initial confusion, I mistakenly assumed she was the TB patient because she came to the clinic every day to get his pills. When I learned her name—and that Lindumzi was a male name and not a female one—I inquired about Lindumzi's health and if he was taking the pills. After all, the idea of Directly Observed Therapy is that the patients are, well, observed taking their pills. NoFirst assured me he was taking the medication and in good health. The numerous other TB patients at Lindumzi's stage of treatment were doing quite well and I assumed he was in similar shape. It was not unusual for a man to find work in town during the day when we were open and send his wife to collect the pills.

Lindumzi and NoFirst had five children, ranging in age from about ten months to eight years. These children made the family stand out to me, particularly the second-youngest, Tununu, who was three years old when I arrived. Because she had been born several weeks prematurely, she was much smaller than her classmates. But she compensated for her small size with an outrageously large ego and sense of self-confidence that was evident in my every interaction with her. While other children in the preschool clambered around me, desperate for any slice of attention, Tununu stayed away, steering around and ignoring the chaos that engulfed my visits to the preschool. Watching her promenade past, sashaying as if she were on a fashion catwalk, I realized that even in shantytowns there were budding prima donnas.

But there were two things that Tununu liked that I could offer her. The first was my camera. Like the other children, she loved to have her picture taken and she easily produced some of my most memorable shots of Itipini. After a few lucky shots, I would occasionally camp out around her with my camera—no doubt feeding her three-year-old ego—and try to get another good one. She was always happy to oblige.

The other thing I could offer her was my guitar. On this point, she deigned to be like the rest of the children and was always eager to dance to any number I played, doing a strange and endearing two-footed hop back and forth to whatever song we happened to be singing. An ongoing challenge in those early months was learning the names of all the preschool students, given the chaos that surrounded each of the visits and the unfamiliar-sounding names. We had added "He's Got the Whole World" to our repertoire and I realized I could insert a child's name for "the whole world," thereby giving a child a moment in the sun and a chance for me to repeat his or her name several times. Tununu loved when I did this for her. She would continue her little dancing hop but stare at me in wonder at the same time.

Lindumzi was a mystery to me for many months, even though he lived closer than most other patients. I was still too new and uncertain of myself to think about seeking him out on my own accord, something that would come naturally later on, so I first met him only when he came up for a two-month review of his treatment and had to provide another sputum sample for a test. It was a good chance to visually check on him and his progress.

When NoFirst took me up to see him, I was shocked at what I found. Lindumzi lay sprawled in his bed, a pile of ragged and fraying blankets on top of him. Next to the bed was an old cloth he was using as his handkerchief, soaked in the mucus and phlegm he coughed up from his lungs as I sat with him. He couldn't walk, he could barely sit up, and he had to take several breaths between each word just to have the energy to speak. Aside from Fumanekile and one or two others, who had gradually deteriorated in front of my eyes on their daily visits, I had only seen asymptomatic HIV-positive people, who looked no different than anyone else. But here, in the back room behind the spaza shop, I saw the AIDS epidemic as it had been portrayed in so many photo-essays in the Western media: gaunt, emaciated, weak, and dying. And it had just been a short walk from the clinic.

I had obviously done a poor job caring for Lindumzi. A patient on TB treatment should never have been allowed to deteriorate this far without our knowledge. Perhaps spurred by this guilt or the connection I felt to his wife and children, I felt a strong attachment to him as one of "my" TB patients. More than that, he was the very picture of the AIDS patients I had moved to Africa to save. Staring at him in the shack, it became my mission to fix this problem and right this wrong.

Even though it was obvious just from looking at him that Lindumzi was eligible for antiretroviral treatment to fight the AIDS, he still needed blood work to measure how much the virus had affected his immune system. For an asymptomatic patient, this CD4 count could be as high as eight hundred or one thousand. The government admitted patients to the ARV program when their count fell below two hundred. Jenny drew the blood that day for Lindumzi's count but the lab still took a week to return the results. It was seventeen, I-can't-believe-you're-still-alive territory.

With this lab result, Lindumzi was ready for ARV preparation, and I was ready to see he made it through. But there was a new obstacle—Lindumzi himself. Dorothy, Jenny's counterpart in the clinic, counseled him about the efficacy and importance of ARVs. But he refused to go to the government clinic, citing myths about the drugs, claiming they wouldn't heal him and saying he would come back when he was "ready." He tottered out, leaning heavily on a cane, and made his way to his back room.

I hadn't anticipated Lindumzi himself being an obstacle to my increasingly fervent desire to save him. But it was so clear—to me—what had to be done. The ARVs would give him strength and prolong his life. With such a low CD4 count, each passing day became a wasted opportunity, and it was unclear how many more he would have. My Xhosa was fractured and pathetic but I visited him in his shack several times, imploring him to begin the process to get the drugs that could prolong his life. I offered him as many rides to the clinic and the hospital as he needed. I explained how the drugs would help him. It didn't change his mind.

Lindumzi's condition didn't improve but neither did it deteriorate as quickly as I anticipated. There were several more opportunities for counseling sessions from Dorothy and impromptu visits from me or Jenny. On one visit, he rearranged his blankets and I was shocked to see how thin he had become. His weigh-ins at the clinic told us he had been losing weight rapidly but his loose-fitting clothes had always hidden the full extent of the weight loss. Now, I realized, I could nearly fit my fingers around his thigh.

Lindumzi's story had a predictable ending; he died in late January at age thirty-two. NoFirst and her children returned to the family's rural village for several weeks for the funeral. When they came back to Itipini, it seemed like things were back to normal. Tununu was back in the preschool smiling for my camera and doing the same dance. NoFirst was still working hard, now dressed in widow's green.

But a few weeks after they returned, she came into the clinic with the classic symptoms of tuberculosis—night sweats, cough, loss of appetite—and when she was tested, she was positive and began another round of treatment. (While signing her up for D.O.T., I learned from her government ID that her first name was Xoliswa and I started calling her that. But she would silence me with a stern "NoFirst!" before breaking into a rare smile. I never learned when or why she had changed her name.)

I wanted to hope for the best for the family but the TB diagnosis was a reminder of NoFirst's mortality and generally poor health. Her CD4 count was up-to-date and showed that the virus was affecting her but not to the point where she qualified for ARVs. There had been a mild decline in her health over the several months I had known her. I couldn't help wondering what would happen if her decline continued and she died as well. When I looked at her children, I thought about all the AIDS orphans I had heard so much about across the continent. I wondered what the phrase was for young children who weren't orphans yet but might someday be.

For several months, though, NoFirst seemed to be doing well. She was regular with her TB pills, her CD4 count stayed respectably high, and her children were attending school. But I couldn't help noticing small changes. The spaza shop wasn't doing as well—in fact, I rarely saw any goods for sale when I chased the children up the hill after preschool. The music seemed less constant, a sign, perhaps, that the *shebeen* was losing out to one of its many rivals in the community. The children seemed less consistently clean and less well dressed. Perhaps the burden of running such a large household on her own was finally wearing NoFirst down.

About halfway through her treatment, NoFirst asked for two weeks of TB pills because she was taking the whole family back to the village. We made sure she would be returning to Itipini—otherwise, we would have had to transfer her treatment to the clinic in her village—but she assured us it would be a short visit. Two weeks passed and they didn't return. Then a month, then two, and there was no sign. I thought of them occasionally and wondered where they had ended up. In the crush of daily patient visits and new HIV clients demanding attention, however, it was hard to focus on a patient who wasn't right in front of us. It wasn't unusual for people to make extended visits to the rural areas. We could only hope that NoFirst had been to the local clinic to continue her treatment.

Two months after NoFirst left, I was idly chatting in Xhosa with a young woman I knew to be a friend of NoFirst's and I mentioned how I missed the family. The young woman switched to halting English: "NoFirst, she has died." The news floored me and I didn't believe it at first, using as many Xhosa words for death as I knew to double check, but the friend just kept nodding. NoFirst had died in her village about two weeks earlier. I asked about the children and the friend said they were staying with NoFirst's mother in the village and would be there indefinitely. I never learned anything more about the circumstances of the death and I never saw Tununu or any of her siblings ever again.

It is one thing to read stories and be seized with urgency about AIDS orphans. But the true heartbreak is to come to know a family—to begin to understand some of the relationships that bind them together, to form memories relating to specific instances with those family members—and then watch its decline as it crumbles apart. NoFirst had leaped into my memory by speaking directly about my role in her life—"I want you." But in the end what had I been able to provide her? How had I justified her need for me? She was still dead and Tununu and her siblings were still Africa's newest AIDS orphans. The incarnational ministry of presence wasn't looking so good. It wasn't easy to simply be present as a person—a friend—deteriorated and died in front of me.

It had been clear to me what kind of care NoFirst and Lindumzi needed—TB treatment, regular vitamins and nutritional supplements, CD4 counts, and eventually ARVs. That was clear to my educated mind. Their illnesses were serious, but the combination of TB and HIV was not uncommon in Itipini and I had seen it successfully treated in numerous other instances. But like Thandeka, this natural and obvious—to me—progression of care was stymied by their own decisions, namely, Lindumzi's decision to delay and avoid ARV preparation and NoFirst's decision to move back to her rural village, far from the care she needed, and presumably default on her treatment for lack of access. Driving home the day I learned of NoFirst's death, I thought how I could have prevented it. Short of forbidding her to return home or tracking her down in her village and dragging her back, neither of which seemed either feasible or appealing to the missionary who was so excited about serving and learning, I didn't know what I could have done. My best efforts had been rendered ineffectual and meaningless.

Missionaries inhabit a delicate position. Generally, by the standards of their sending society, missionaries are better educated, better connected, and better off than the people they go to help. Together, this makes missionaries more powerful than those being served. But the people they go to help have not traditionally invited the missionaries to come to their homes. Rather, missionaries have decided to take their power and put it in service to those without. Many missionaries are motivated by a deep desire to enable local people to make their own decisions about their own lives.

When these impulses come in conflict, there's a clear solution: put one's talents and skills in service to others and, equally, learn from them. If missionaries build up the power and education of the people they serve, then those people will be able to make decisions on the basis of the same knowledge as the missionaries, informed by their local context and understandings. This is why education is so important and why "empowerment" and "capacity building" are justifiably buzzwords. We spent time on Friday mornings, in private conversation, and whenever the opportunity arose to build up the knowledge of the people in Itipini so that when they confronted future challenges they would better be able to handle them.

The trouble is that effective education and true empowerment take enormous amounts of time, and often there are preexisting—and incorrect—assumptions that need to be broken down and overcome. HIV, TB, and burns killed much faster than we could educate, leaving us in an uncomfortable position. Either we mandated behavior to people whose guests we were, with the likely result that the mandate would be ignored, or we let people make their own decisions and watched the predictable results unfold, powerless to stop them. We had done our best to muddle through. The end result of that muddling was that we stood by ineffectually as preventable deaths unfolded before our eyes.

The aphorism "Give me a fish, feed me for a day; teach me to fish, feed me for a lifetime" is well known. But it has nothing to say about how long it takes to teach someone to fish or about what can be done in the interim period until they have made that knowledge their own. "Live and learn" is often used to exculpate ourselves from situations where we've tried to teach someone but made no progress. Thinking about the deaths of Thandeka, Lindumzi, and NoFirst, I was left asking, "But what happens if they don't live?"

Eight

Graveyard Traffic Jam

LINDUMZI, NOFIRST, AND THANDEKA had known about the kind of help we could offer them in the clinic and had more or less turned it down—intentionally, in the case of Lindumzi, less so in the case of NoFirst. If they didn't want our help, there was only so much we could do for them without imposing our will and denying them control of their health. Sizeka was a different case. She came looking for our help. But she came too late.

It was a May morning when Sizeka came into the clinic. I had been in Itipini for nine months, my Xhosa was improving—I could now successfully make the x-click—and I had notified my bosses at the Episcopal Church that I was planning to stay on for a second year. There were still daily frustrations—children still crawled all over me, for instance—but I was beginning to see why and how people might keep being missionaries year after year.

Sizeka's friends later told me she had been beautiful before she got sick, one of the most beautiful girls her age. But when I first saw her that morning, she was emaciated, weak, and pale, and had no energy to walk, eat, or care for herself. As a result, her long hair had a wild look and her thin face was stretched taut against her cheekbones. Though she was only twenty-two, she could have been forty. Looking at her leaning against the doorjamb, struggling for breath, it was clear that the walk from her shack to the clinic had been far too much.

This visit to the clinic was Sizeka's first in over a year. When I looked at her medical records, I saw she had tested positive for HIV several years earlier. But it had been more than eighteen months since she had last had a CD4 count, the crucial measure of how HIV had affected her immune system and the single most important factor that would determine if she was eligible to begin the lengthy preparation process for the life-prolonging antiretroviral drugs. It was those same drugs that Lindumzi had declined to take and that Fumanekile had started trying to get before he had died. Jenny was full of stories of people who had been at death's door, made it through the preparation process for ARVs, and returned to full health such that their previous health condition was barely noticeable. But I had yet to see anyone do that.

The South African government admits patients to antiretroviral treatment when their CD4 count falls below two hundred. (In the United States, many health programs start treatment when it falls below 350.) But before they can start taking the pills, each patient has to go through a lengthy preparation process that can take, at a minimum, four weeks, accompanied by a friend or family member, called a treatment support partner, who ensures they adhere to the treatment. In many ways, this makes sense. Once they start, patients will have to take ARVs every day for the rest of their life. They need to know what they are committing to and the importance of being consistent with the treatment. But as I learned with Fumanekile, the preparation process can stretch on interminably, and people can—and do—die before they receive the pills. It was too complicated to administer ARVs in Itipini so we referred all our patients to the government health center in Ngangalizwe, the township up the hill behind Itipini.

So that patients can start treatment as soon as their CD4 counts dip below two hundred, the guidelines call for a CD4 count every six months for HIV positive patients. That way, patients can start preparation while they are still relatively strong and able to navigate the system by themselves. Sizeka's records showed that her CD4 count eighteen months earlier had been just on the high side of two hundred. If she had followed up with another count six months later, she almost certainly would have been below two hundred and therefore able to start preparation then.

But that was all past. Here she was, seemingly on the verge of death, and she hadn't even begun the ARV process. Jenny drew the blood for the CD4 count and I drove Sizeka and her blood sample to the Ngangalizwe health center, accompanied by Sizeka's childhood friend Noxolo, the young woman who had also accompanied me when Fumanekile was so sick and who now volunteered to support Sizeka in the process. At the health center, we encountered a new problem. Sizeka had lost her government-issued ID, without which the nurses were reluctant to begin treatment or send her blood to the lab. There had been cases of ARV fraud in the past and the nurses wanted to be sure the paperwork was right. I had come to know several of the nurses quite well, and while Sizeka sat on the bench slumped against Noxolo and in no condition to commit fraud of any kind, I vouched for her identity and prayed the nurses would show a little flexibility. Even with my best Xhosa and a winning smile, they didn't. Deviation from the guidelines proved impossible.

Later, after we helped Sizeka back to her shack with promises to sort out the ID the next day, Noxolo and I took a break in a small side room in the Community Project and aired our frustration to each other. Noxolo's English was good and my Xhosa was improving so we talked in a mix of the two, criticizing the nurses for their inaction. Noxolo, understandably angry that no one was helping her obviously sick friend, concluded, in perfect English, "They are not nurses. They are murderers. They are letting her die." Leaning against the cool cement wall, it was hard to disagree.

Venting our emotion didn't do anything to make Sizeka better. The next day Noxolo and I loaded Sizeka in the *bakkie* and headed into town in search of an ID. Our plan was relatively straightforward: get an ID photo from the local pharmacy and take it to the Department of Home Affairs to get the temporary replacement, which could be printed while we waited. Sizeka could barely walk and there was no parking near the pharmacy so I had to park down the street. Noxolo hopped out and helped Sizeka out of the *bakkie*. Sizeka immediately slumped against Noxolo, her much taller frame enveloping short Noxolo. Noxolo maneuvered Sizeka until she was against her side and the two set out along the sidewalk, the stream of people on the pavement parting smoothly to let them pass without looking at either of them. They inched along, each step a major undertaking for Sizeka.

I hung back. I had no doubt Noxolo could handle the situation on her own. Moreover, I reasoned, it really was better for me to lessen my involvement in the situation so as to increase the role of local people in solving their own problems. But the truth was it made me uncomfortable to think about walking down the street with Sizeka. I already drew enough stares when I walked through Mthatha simply for being white. I wasn't prepared for how I imagined those stares would intensify if I walked along with an obviously sick black woman on my arm. Incarnational ministry was fine in Itipini where everyone knew who I was and didn't look at me oddly. But in downtown Mthatha, the idea of incarnation was a little bit harder to swallow. I wanted Sizeka to be saved, but in this instance I was happy for someone else to do the saving. So I stayed a few steps behind, pretending I was busy reading the posters on the sidewalk or looking at what the street vendors had for sale.

A short while later, photo in hand, Noxolo and Sizeka shuffled along to the Department of Home Affairs, the same place I had brought the high school students some months before. Even with Noxolo's sweet talk to the security guards that allowed them to skip the legendarily long lines, it was still two hours before Sizeka had a new ID in hand, two hours she spent slumped on the bench, barely conscious of what was going on around her. With her ID in hand, we returned to Ngangalizwe and dropped off her blood sample to be tested.

When the results came back a week later, they were forty-four—well below the two hundred mark that qualified her for ARVs and a reminder, if we needed one, that Sizeka might not have much longer to live. In the week we waited, Sizeka's condition continued to deteriorate. She couldn't keep down any food at all and became dehydrated and even weaker as a result. When we arrived for her ARV appointments, the nurses saw how sick she was and started treating her symptoms. Sizeka lay on a stretcher with an IV in her arm looking miserable before being sent home marginally stronger but with no progress made on getting the ARV prescription. Eventually, the health center just referred her to the hospital for more advanced care. By this point, she couldn't walk at all.

Mthatha General Hospital had a crush of similar cases, many more immediate and acute than Sizeka's general and gradual decline. When we arrived, she would get easily lost in the shuffle on the stretcher in a busy hallway. When I had been here with Fumanekile, I had jumped the line of patients waiting in the hallway. Sizeka's condition was an emergency, but at least she was conscious—barely—so it was a modestly less acute situation than Fumanekile's. So we waited, Noxolo, Sizeka, and me. Sometimes I left to return to work at the clinic. When Sizeka was treated, the nurses often had to put the IV in her neck because it was no longer possible to get at the veins in her arms. The doctor would prescribe vitamins and anti-vomiting pills and tell her to continue ARV preparation. The pills did little good, however, because they didn't address the underlying causes of her illness.

Noxolo and Sizeka finished one visit to the hospital earlier than I anticipated. Rather than waiting for me to come get them, Noxolo decided the two of them could take a taxi back to Itipini. The nearest place to Itipini a taxi would stop was a mile away in front of one of Mthatha's malls. Noxolo left Sizeka there and walked back to Itipini to ask me for a ride the rest of the way. Climbing into Jenny's *bakkie*, we went to pick her up.

The taxi rank where Sizeka was waiting was one of the busiest places in town. The taxis alone generate chaos as they pull in and out of the parking lot. They are surrounded by scores of street vendors hawking assorted goods and women sitting in front of fruit and sweet stands. The mall is ringed by grocery stores and gas stations and the sheer volume of people passing through that area at any given moment is overwhelming. Because municipal services in Mthatha aren't always perfect, the parking lot is ringed by trash, some of it gathered in piles, some scattered aimlessly.

Noxolo pointed away from the taxis to a far edge of the lot and we walked over. I don't know what I was expecting to see—perhaps Sizeka sitting against a wall someplace—but it wasn't what I got. Sizeka was lying behind a gas station, on the edge of the parking lot, in the midst of a pile of garbage, covered in a thick blanket, though, as it was late summer, it was one of the hottest days I had then experienced. Here, on the edge of a busy parking lot, surrounded by swarms of people moving in different directions, was one young woman, dying alone on a pile of garbage.

Noxolo made it to Sizeka first, helped her to her feet, and supported her as they started back for the *bakkie*. Watching them struggle and thinking about how Sizeka had been waiting on a pile of garbage for me, my previous concerns about being white in such a crowded and unfamiliar place disappeared. I walked over and told Sizeka to lean back in my arms. She fell more than leaned, and I carried her, like a groom carrying his new bride, through the gas station, across the parking lot and back to the *bakkie*. I am not a strong person. But she was so thin that it wasn't a struggle. The only pain I felt came with each step as her hip bone, stripped of its protective fat, jammed into my abdomen.

We had a small sick bay in a spare room at the Community Project and when we returned to Itipini I took her there. She was a burden for her family in their little shack. In the sick bay a few designated staff could look after her and bring her food. But it was only a palliative measure. The real cure—and I was convinced there still was one even if the process was going slower than I might have liked—would have to come from the medical system. But the never-ending circle of treatment didn't actually seem to be improving her condition.

When I went to check on her each morning to make sure she was ready for that day's trip to the health center or the hospital, I could sense her anticipation: perhaps this trip would be the one that would finally deal with her illness. It was a touching—and misplaced—faith in the efficacy and speediness of medical science. But it was that anticipation and faith that gave her the energy to get out of bed, wash herself, and be helped into the *bakkie*. But then each time she threw up whatever new pills she had been given, I could see the despair set in again and the hope that motivated her in the morning fade away. The question was written plainly on her face: will I make it through this alive? With each passing appointment that failed to change her condition, the will to get up and out of bed—the will to live—slowly drained away.

On our drives home, Sizeka, her hair wildly arrayed around her, leaned against Noxolo's shoulder, crying silent tears that leaked down her sunken face. I glanced at Noxolo and wondered what it would be like to have someone you played with as a child and sat next to in school deteriorate to such a point. Noxolo simply held her close and sang softly to her. It was more than I could manage. I wanted to give Sizeka a pep talk and tell her how she just needed to persevere a little longer and get ARVs and how they would strengthen her. But I lacked the vocabulary for this, and even the peppiest of talks would have made little dent in Sizeka's mood of increasing despair.

To this point, my mission efforts had been rooted in the idea of presence. Given all the obstacles to actually doing anything—all these car rides with no pills to show for it were one example—showing up, sharing an existence, and being present were all I had going for me. I tried to remind myself on these car rides with Sizeka that simply being with her at a difficult time—even if I didn't say anything—was a meaningful and valuable ministry. But it was wholly unsatisfying. Here was a woman who was clearly suffering and I could do nothing at all for her aside from a mere ride. No matter what I told myself, I still seemed to be making a weak stab at ministry. Presence, I was learning, is paradoxical. It's the easiest form of ministry there is. Yet it is one impossibly difficult to bear.

I kept returning to the stories Jenny had told me about other patients who had come back from the brink of death once they were on ARVs. That hope kept me going. I began to believe that Sizeka would be the latest such addition to the list of people who had made it back from being near death's door. She would be a story of my own I could tell future visitors. I let myself imagine how I would casually chat with Sizeka when she was stronger, maybe as she waited at the faucet for water or before morning prayers.

She died on a Monday morning, about a week after she went into the sick bay and just moments before we showed up to open the clinic that morning.

⁊

In a culture where HIV is so prevalent, it is difficult to understand how adjusted people become to death. When I picked up Dorothy for work on Monday mornings, I always made sure to ask about her weekend. But I tired of this when I realized her answer was always some variation of, "I was at a funeral on Saturday." Seemingly every weekend, someone she knew or was related to was being buried. One Monday morning, I changed my question and asked if she had been to a funeral on Saturday. She hadn't, she said, with a sort of furtive look, and explained, "Sometimes there are too many funerals to go to. You can't get anything done for yourself. I snuck around town on Saturday and did my errands and hoped no one saw me."

Still, I didn't quite grasp how deeply death has changed the way of life until I went to Sizeka's funeral, the first I had been to for someone from Itipini. The funeral service itself was broadly similar to what I might have expected back home. Songs were sung, people spoke of their memories of Sizeka, and a priest said a few prayers. It was in Xhosa so I didn't understand all of it but it seemed a fitting homage to someone who had died so young. At the end we gathered around the coffin for one final look at Sizeka. I wasn't eager to see her again but I was jostled closest to the casket and couldn't avoid looking down on her face. She was different than I remembered her. Her eyes were still sunk and the skin stretched taut across her face but I finally saw a hint of the beauty everyone had mentioned—high cheekbones, hair neatly arranged, and a graceful chin.

We loaded into a rented taxi, the hearse, and my little car and set out for the graveyard. This too was familiar to me. I put on my hazard lights and followed the hearse at about half the speed limit. Even Mthatha's notoriously difficult traffic seemed to get out of the way for our little procession. But the situation changed dramatically when we pulled into the graveyard. There were cars everywhere. We only had three in our procession but there were scores waiting, some trying to get out from the previous funerals and some trying to get in, like us, for other funerals going on at the same time. I woke up from the mindless doze of the drive and had to start paying attention. Even so, it was quite a few minutes before we were parked. I was used to running into snarled traffic jams in downtown Mthatha. To find one even at the graveyard was a surprise.

What struck me first about the Mthatha public cemetery was all the fresh soil. With so many burials every week, the soil was being constantly disturbed and turned. There was no time for grass to grow, let alone be trimmed and cared for. Instead of a neat and tidy expanse of green, all I could see was pale brown, sometimes in mounds over fresh graves, sometimes in big dirt piles next to the empty ones. As we walked to the graveside, I realized I didn't know which grave we were heading to. There were too many holes in the ground. There were so many burials taking place on that particular Saturday that there were a dozen or so empty graves lined up. There was no more than twelve inches between the graves, and the rows were separated by about two feet. Walking past the empty graves, I immediately remembered a book I had recently finished about the Rwandan genocide and a phrase made infamous by the Hutu Power movement—"the graves are not yet full."

The context was different but the idea of a constant and overwhelming stream of death was similar.

We gathered around the hole that had been chosen for Sizeka and prepared for her final graveside rites. On one side was a big pile of dirt, ready to be shoveled on top of Sizeka the moment we were done. On the other side was another row of graves. Somehow, we found the space to cram the fifteen or so of us in the twelve inches along each side of Sizeka's final resting place, some of us perched more precariously than others as we tried to avoid falling into one of the empty graves before our time. A few women began singing as the coffin was lowered down.

But not four feet away, the previous funeral was just finishing up. A group of men were shoveling the grave full, chitchatting among themselves as they did. Six feet behind us, on the other side of the next row of graves, a funeral home employee was setting up a tent for the next funeral, clanging together the metal pipes and unwrapping the tent. About 150 feet away, at another row of graves, another, larger, funeral was going on simultaneously. They had a sound system so we could hear everything they said. That was the soundtrack for Sizeka's funeral—the shoveling of dirt, the setting up of a tent, another service, and muted singing from our group.

In this context, the graveside service for Sizeka was rather more perfunctory and lacking in dignity than what I generally expect to be accorded these sorts of events. The casket was arranged, prayers were muttered, songs were sung, dirt was tossed, and we all went to wait in the car while the men in the group stayed back, shoveling the grave full.

✑

Just a few days after the funeral, an older woman named Phatiswa came into the clinic clutching a paper bag tightly in her hands. The paper bag held three bottles of antiretroviral drugs she had just been prescribed. She had come to alert us to this development in her care. We applauded the news and thanked her for informing us. When I noted the ARVs in her medical records, it was a shock to see just how quickly and dramatically her life had changed. She had tested positive for HIV on April 10. Her CD4 count results—116—were returned on April 24. She immediately began the preparation process and a little more than a month later—June 5—she walked into the clinic to show us the pills. Our role at the clinic had been minimal. We did the initial HIV test and helped her to the hospital for a required chest x-ray. Otherwise, she had acted completely of her own volition. The impetus during the entire process had been her own.

Noxolo's comment about letting Sizeka die had rung true for me at the time. But as I thought about Sizeka's last weeks in light of Phatiswa I wondered what role Sizeka had played—or not played—in her own health care. It's unkind to be uncharitable about the dead but I wondered how the situation would have been different if Sizeka had that CD4 count when it was due a year before her death. She would have been stronger and better able to fend for herself and wouldn't have needed much help from me at all. She could have walked to the Ngangalizwe health center on her own and navigated the ARV preparation process as easily as Phatiswa had. Instead, she had waited until her CD4 count was forty-four to come looking for help. By then, she was perched precariously on the edge of life and death. Our efforts were too little and too late.

Her health had been routinely and comprehensively neglected in a way that boggled my mind. But what explained the situation? Was it apathy? Denial about her condition? Ignorance of her options? For Sizeka, it was likely some mix of the three, no doubt abetted by the generalized, though weakening, stigma associated with HIV. Plainly, governments and aid organizations can pay for ARV programs. Much of the money for the ARVs that patients in Itipini were getting came from the United States President's Emergency Plan for AIDS Relief, started by George W. Bush. But no matter how well funded these programs were, the money alone wouldn't solve the problem. There needed to be some sort of education component to go with it so that people would know the importance of, for instance, regular CD4 counts. And, indeed, I saw billboards and heard the radio spots all the time. Clearly, however, it was not reaching everyone.

The people I knew who took to ARVs most quickly were those whose friends and role models were talking openly about the importance of taking the pills. That wasn't a surprise. But it was less clear what my role should be. Sizeka was not the only person in Itipini long overdue for a CD4 count. A basic part of my missionary outlook, however, was the belief in empowerment and helping people do things for themselves. Was it my job to seek these overdue people out, drag them to the clinic, and make them get a count? At the very least, that would take energy from my other efforts, such as helping people like Sizeka who had waited too long. It seemed paternalistic and offensive to believe that I knew more about their health than they did. But I did. Sizeka's death proved that.

We tried to strike a balance in the clinic. We never played CD4 count truant officer but we also didn't let people pass by unnoticed. Whenever patients who were HIV positive came in to the clinic for whatever reason, we checked to see when their last CD4 count had been and offered to draw blood if the time was right. But a common response was "ngomso," meaning "tomorrow," which turned into next week, next month, never. Moreover, it missed a big chunk of people, mainly men, who rarely darkened the door of the clinic until they were as sick as Sizeka had been. We talked publicly and openly and counseled patients about the importance of ARVs but it clearly wasn't trickling down as we wanted it to. Was it right to keep spending time urging people to get CD4 counts? Or should we sigh and turn to the next patient in the always long line of people waiting to be seen?

&

Before she died, Sizeka had been living with her aunt, an older woman named Nosipho, who was also HIV positive and had a CD4 count just below two hundred, making her eligible for ARVs. When we talked about it in Sizeka's last weeks, she had declined to begin the process. It seemed a reasonable decision at the time. She was reasonably healthy and was spending all her time caring for her niece. Shortly after Sizeka's funeral, however, I cornered Nosipho after morning prayer. Now was her chance, I explained. I'd be happy to drive her up to Ngangalizwe any time she wanted so she could begin the ARV preparation. She had just seen her niece die. Surely, she wanted to begin now to avoid a similar fate?

Nosipho shook her head. "I don't have a friend," she said, meaning she didn't have someone willing to be her treatment support partner. That wasn't good enough for me. She had lived in Itipini for some time. Surely there was someone—boyfriend, sister, daughter—who could spare the time?

"My sister is coming next week from the rural areas," she said. "She'll go with me."

I let the matter lie there for a week or two and when I checked again Nosipho hadn't made the first visit. "My sister is coming next week," she said. "I'll go then."

Nosipho wasn't often around the Community Project area and my other responsibilities meant we didn't run into each other often. But every few weeks, I made sure to check on her. Her sister had never shown up—if she had ever been coming—and Nosipho still hadn't begun treatment. She seemed to labor a little harder to carry water and she was losing weight. In the past, we had sent staff members along with people who couldn't find a treatment support partner, and I offered to arrange the same for Nosipho. She declined.

Months passed and Nosipho still didn't begin the ARV process. Her health had stabilized. It wasn't great but she also wasn't at death's door. More than a year after Sizeka's death, on my last day in Itipini, I visited Nosipho one last time in her shack. She was sitting outside, washing clothes. I rehearsed all the familiar lines about the importance of ARVs. She smiled and nodded and didn't say much. My best pleas were meaningless.

I knew many more people like Sizeka and Nosipho in Itipini, people who failed to grasp that HIV is a life-changing diagnosis and waited until it was too late before they sought our help. But I also knew some like Phatiswa, who listened to the counseling from Dorothy at the time of her test and got right to work on ARVs. Despite our best efforts at education, we still had far more Nosiphos and Sizekas than Phatiswas. I was resolved to change that. I didn't know how many more Sizekas I could handle.

Nine

Let's Talk About . . . Sex?

THE CROWD OF YOUNG mothers continued to giggle and flirt with me on Tuesdays in the clinic. But there was still a degree of respect. My skin color created a distance between us. As the white biker gang that first night in East London had been able to expect not to be challenged by the black waitstaff, so long as my skin color was the primary part of my identity, I received a similar sort of deference.

But Vuyelwa stood out. Even though she was just seventeen when I met her, she was unencumbered by any such distance. When she came into the clinic, she made it clear what she wanted and expected me to help her get it. This could make her seem demanding at times but it also gave her a spark and vitality, and I looked forward to seeing her. Her infant son, Bulumko, had been an unplanned child, as most were in Itipini, but she doted over him and was clearly prepared to make the best go she could of motherhood, something I couldn't say for all the other young mothers. Best of all, her English, while far from fluent, was good enough that we could speak English almost exclusively, giving me a welcome break from Xhosa.

I often saw Vuyelwa in the kitchen where she was visiting her mother, the woman everyone called Wee Mama, who had been one of the cooks at the Project for as long as Jenny had been around. Wee Mama had made herself my surrogate mother, welcoming me into the kitchen when I wanted a break and always forcing food on me at lunchtime. Although Vuyelwa flirted with me like all the other young mothers and

I probably returned the attention, the connection to Wee Mama made it easy—for me—to think about Vuyelwa in a sisterly sort of way.

As a result, it was sometimes easy to think of her as relatively close in age to me. I saw her working around their house, cooking and washing. She showed an early interest in the library and liked to read out loud to me when I had the time. But she was also clearly seventeen. She could be pouty and petulant, like any teenager, when she didn't get her way. She insisted on looking as good as she could, even though she only had a few pieces of nice clothing and so wore them all the time. One yellow tank top made at least three appearances a week.

Still, we didn't see each other all that often—she had chores to do and went to town—and I was occupied with other things. So it was a surprise one morning when she asked to come along when I drove a patient to the hospital. It was an unusual request but I agreed. Bulumko was in the kitchen with Wee Mama and Vuyelwa seemed like she was just looking for something to break the monotony of the day. I looked forward to the company.

After we dropped the patient off and were headed back to Itipini, she asked me, "Jesse, do you know what a *tsotsi* is?"

"Sure," I said. "It's a gangster or a thug." The wandering gangs of young men I saw in Itipini could be quite friendly with me, I knew, especially when they were drunk and hanging around the *shebeens*. But I knew it was these same young men who were responsible for much of the crime in Itipini that happened after Jenny and I left for the day.

"Last night a *tsotsi* came into our house and he tried to rape me. He broke down the door, pulled a knife, told me to be quiet, and held me down. I screamed and he punched me but I held him like this"—she demonstrated holding someone tightly to her chest—"and Bantu"—her brother—"ran in and scared him away." It was a gripping story, told in her halting English. I hated my first reaction to it.

"Oh, well," I thought to myself. "What are you going to do? At least he didn't succeed."

I promptly gave myself a mental smack. Here was a person who was becoming as close as any other to me and my only reaction was a cavalier lack of sympathy for an attempted rape. Desperate for something appropriate to say in response, I reached for the lessons I had been taught as a camp counselor to deal with disclosures of sexual abuse: be as affirming as possible, thank her for telling me the story, and tell her that what happened was wrong. When I said that, her exasperated response was simply, "I know!" I told her that when we returned to the clinic, she should talk to Dorothy or Jenny, but other than a small bruise from the punch on her face, there wasn't any visible sign of the altercation. Physically, she would be fine.

That she told me the story was, in many ways, a sign of my increasing enmeshment in the community. But the boundaries were falling faster than I was prepared for. I wanted to be present and share an existence with people. But I also wanted to be in control of that process. My lack of sympathy when she told me the story was a defensive reaction to prevent myself from entering too deeply into the moment. Still, I was grateful she had chosen to confide this news in me. I only wished that my comfort level with the situations people put to me was increasing at the same pace.

The conversation also opened up a new topic for the first time: sex. It was at the center of much of our patient care but I had struggled to find a way to address it. Haltingly and gently, I steered the conversation away from Vuyelwa's disclosure and in the direction of her HIV status. But even that question can be asked without direct reference to HIV or sex. "Do you know your status?" I asked, and she obviously knew, as others always did, that I was referring to her HIV status.

"Negative," she replied with obvious relief and a certain note of finality in her voice.

"When were you tested?"

"When Bulumko was born." Mothers who attend the government antenatal clinic are encouraged to be tested for HIV to determine if they should take nevirapine, the drug that sharply reduces the chance of mother-to-child transmission of HIV during childbirth.

"Vuyelwa," I said, "that was ten months ago. You should be tested more frequently than that. Come to the clinic and have a test soon."

Vuyelwa responded with a one-word Xhosa phrase: "Ndinoyika"— "I am afraid."

Though I would come to expect this response, it surprised me to hear it from Vuyelwa. "Why? It's better to know your status than not to know," I said, repeating a line I would use over and over again in similar situations in the future.

"But I don't want to be positive. And I am afraid to learn the results. What if I am positive? What will happen then?"

It was surprising and disappointing that Vuyelwa was asking these questions. Public health education campaigns designed to combat HIV focused on the importance of testing, knowing one's status, and the availability of antiretroviral drugs that could prolong the lives of people with HIV. As with Sizeka or Lindumzi, the message hadn't trickled down to Vuyelwa in any meaningful way. I patiently explained all these things to her but I could tell from her expression and body language that my message wasn't getting through.

I was torn. I had barely begun to delve into uncharted territory and there was so much more that I wanted to know—did she use condoms? did she have just one sexual partner?—but it was difficult to know how to extend the conversation without seeming prurient or raising issues that only made me uncomfortable. Vuyelwa was a young woman and I a young man. Whatever the extent of our friendship, I was worried that pressing the subject of sex further might be interpreted as a willingness to have sex and not as what it was, a genuine interest in learning more about this aspect of life in Itipini. Our relationship was complicated enough without giving even the hint that sex might be a possibility. It wasn't and wouldn't be. In any event, the conversation had petered out and we were almost back in Itipini.

I had met Sizeka too late in her life to make any meaningful interventions in her life. It was clear that if I wanted to start helping people when it really mattered—rather than watching as they died helplessly in front of me—I needed to be involved in their lives at an earlier point. It was also clear that this meant talking about sex. The main means of transmission of HIV in Itipini and throughout sub-Saharan Africa is heterosexual intercourse. Every time I encountered young mothers or HIV-positive patients the common act that was at the root of their situations was inescapable and yet went largely undiscussed. Honest engagement with the community would require addressing the subject of sex in a truthful and gentle way.

Given the size of the shacks in Itipini, there wasn't a lot of privacy associated with sex either. My friend Noxolo had been raised by her aunt and told me once how when she was seven she had woken up in the middle of the night to find her aunt and boyfriend in the next bed over.

This was not unusual, but the sound her aunt was making was. "Auntie, why are you moaning?" Noxolo asked. "Are you sick?" For that, she had been smacked and told to go back to sleep. Sex was a reality for all ages, not something that happened in bedrooms far from children's eyes.

Yet I had been through years of "safe church" training and I remembered how awkward those sessions about "good touch, bad touch" had been. The implicit message I took away from those years of training was that the best thing to do was to avoid the subject of sex altogether and, if it was ever raised, look for ways to change the subject as quickly as possible. American churches, I had learned, are terrified of sex.

Beyond my own reluctance to discuss sex, it seemed there was a general reluctance to talk openly about sex—especially as it pertained to HIV—in South Africa. When I traveled in Uganda to visit a friend, I was surprised at the frankness of the billboards. "Don't be a sugar daddy," a common one said. "Stop cross-generational sex." By contrast, the billboards in South Africa were relatively anodyne and confusing. "The Got Ambition Generation—Be a part of it!" said one. Somewhere on the sign was a small reference to HIV.

The South African case was compounded by Thabo Mbeki, the second post-apartheid president, who associated himself with fringe scientists and denied that HIV caused AIDS. His judgment and leadership on the AIDS issue was appalling and is widely considered to have led to hundreds of thousands of needless deaths. Yet his views pointed to the complicated relationship between sex, HIV, race, and the history of oppression in Africa. Mbeki, perhaps, didn't want Africans to be cast as suffering a cruel epidemic simply because of uncontrolled libido. That made it easy for non-Africans to blame the epidemic on African sexual behavior and overlook the history of oppression and exploitation that had provided fertile ground for the epidemic to spread.

I never heard anyone in Itipini discuss Mbeki's views on HIV or point to the misleading advice of his health minister that a traditional diet could help alleviate the suffering. But there was undoubtedly a stigma associated with HIV, as if somehow people who had HIV were at fault simply because they had had sex. The stigma was clear in Vuyelwa's fear at having a test. It contributed, no doubt, to Sizeka's failure to have regular CD4 counts. It produced a general reluctance to talk about sex in a meaningful and honest way. A whole new crop of words and phrases had been developed to refer to HIV indirectly. A popular one was to call it "amagama mathathu," "the three letters," and hold up three fingers at the same time to signify the disease. At a World AIDS Day celebration I organized in Itipini, I asked how many people knew someone with HIV. I was the only one who raised my hand. Incredulous, I asked again. A few tentative hands went up and were as quickly taken down.

When I did hear sex discussed openly, it was often in the context of abstinence. People were comfortable discussing sex so long as it was the absence of sex that was at issue. I once heard the local bishop announce to a group of young confirmands that he had a cure for the HIV epidemic. Yes, he admitted, it was shocking news that a man like the bishop of Mthatha could have developed a cure when so many others had not. "The solution," he said, "is easy. The solution is abstinence." Later, I heard another sermon in which the priest led the congregation in a chant, "boys, zip up your pants; girls, cross your legs," complete with hand gestures. And they were right. If everyone abstained from sex, the growth of the epidemic would quickly diminish almost to zero. But it was hopelessly unrealistic. I saw the young mothers in the clinic. I knew young teenagers were complaining of sexually transmitted infections. No matter how well intentioned people can be, lessons learned on Sundays have a way of evaporating in the heat of the moment.

Short of abstinence, the next step most frequently suggested to curb the HIV epidemic is to be faithful to one partner. This is suggested by the A-B-C rubric—abstain, be faithful, use condoms—which was popular in governmental aid circles and the schema we used to counsel patients in the clinic. But faithfulness is not determined by one member in a relationship but by both. A woman can have sex only with her husband or boyfriend, but if he has another girlfriend somewhere else, she may contract HIV despite her decision to remain faithful. In the clinic, we had separate cards to keep track of sexually transmitted infections, and we were especially careful to note the partner of the patient with an STI to ensure the partner came in for medication as well. Reading the cards over time, it was clear that many patients were not remaining faithful to one person.

Economic conditions can also prove an obstacle to faithfulness, something I encountered while driving home from Bible study one cold winter evening. I stopped to pick up a woman who looked like a hitchhiker and asked where she was going.

"Your place," she responded quietly and shyly.

I thought I had misheard her Xhosa and asked again.

"Your house," she said, confused as to why I hadn't understood.

I started naming neighborhoods along the road but she kept shaking her head. It was then I noticed she was dressed rather revealingly for such a cold evening and the pieces began to fall into place in my head. Fortunately, I hadn't started driving away yet so I apologized for the confusion and asked her politely to get out of the car. I drove away thinking about the irony of picking up a prostitute on the way home from Bible study. Transactional sex, whether it involved the explicit exchange of money or the implicit rewarding of "girlfriends" with gifts, was not uncommon.

The final leg of the prevention strategy is to promote the use of condoms. We had in the clinic a large jar of condoms—both male and female—that we ensured was always full, and patients frequently helped themselves. But it was often the same patients over time and many of them had already been infected. The young people—the ones who were getting pregnant and were reluctant to be tested for HIV—never voluntarily took condoms. Encouraging people to take condoms opened up for me all the awkwardness of discussing sex. As a result, when I first tried to distribute condoms, it turned into a hurried process, in which I handed the package over as quickly as possible and with little conversation.

There was one final factor compounding my reluctance to discuss the subject: the language barrier. Talking about sex requires a sensitivity that not everyone possesses in their native language. I had barely made my way through one conversation, almost exclusively in English, with Vuyelwa. It was easy to be further paralyzed into inaction when I began to consider how to bring up the idea of sex in a language I barely spoke. How would I begin to learn the proper vocabulary so as to discuss the topic in appropriately respectful but not distantly medical terms? Language guides contain a wealth of information on basic vocabulary for, say, the kitchen or store but contain precious little about sexual anatomy or sexual acts.

It was in this environment that I realized just how important talking about sex was if I wanted to engage fully with the community, yet also how difficult a task it would be. I was still puzzling over how to advance the conversation with Vuyelwa and encourage her to have another

HIV test when events intervened that opened up a new way to consider the subject.

*

In the midst of a typically busy day at the clinic, Dorothy told me that she had a patient who wanted an HIV test. Because Jenny was out of town, Dorothy wanted to make sure I would do the test after she had given the patient the required pretest counseling. The rapid HIV test only requires a finger-stick similar to the blood sugar test I had learned as an EMT and I frequently did them in Jenny's absence. It was no different on this day, and I told Dorothy to send the patient over and I'd be with her in a minute.

When I turned to see who it was, I was surprised and discomfited to see Luleka, one of the high school students who'd been in regular attendance at my after-school English class. Not only had she been regular in her attendance, she had shown the seeds of a potential that far outstripped her peers, as well as a general sullenness about learning that prevented her from realizing that potential. On this day, she was skipping school, complaining of a headache or a toothache or a cough or any other ailment that would let her take a day off. For some reason, she had also decided she wanted an HIV test. As I hadn't actually checked for tests when I answered Dorothy, I only then realized we were out of them. That meant Luleka would have to walk up to the Ngangalizwe health center. I told her to come back with the results so we could note them in her health records.

I thought about her nearly the whole time she was gone. HIV tests were generally nerve-wracking procedures for me—though I imagine more so for the patient. The instructions said to wait fifteen minutes before reading the test, but I would always peek over several times before the timer rang to see if one (negative) or two (positive) lines appeared on the test strip. But I'd never known any of the patients as well as I knew Luleka. She'd only want the test, I reasoned, if she'd had sex recently, and that raised a number of other questions. Had the sex been consensual? Should she have a pregnancy test? Did she have condoms and know how to use them? As usual, just thinking about these questions made me uncomfortable, though it didn't diminish my belief that they needed to be raised.

She came back forty-five minutes later, sat down, and put a folded piece of paper on the table. It was only because I was busy bandaging a deep gash on another patient's leg that I didn't immediately snatch it from her hands, though I desperately wanted to strip off my gloves and check it. When I finally flipped open her results, my eye immediately went to one word, "Negative." I gave her a big smile and offered her some condoms, trying not to let on just how relieved I was. She grunted a little to show her relief, took the condoms, and walked out.

Even before Luleka's test, I had begun to realize that my English class provided a natural venue to begin discussing sex. Three of the initial five students were mothers and most of them came to the clinic regularly for birth control injections. They were as exposed as any of their peers to sex-related issues. But the obstacles were steep. Not only was the general cultural attitude opposed to the idea of discussing sex, there was the dynamic between us. I was a well-educated, white male and they were poorly educated, black women. The balance of power— economically and educationally—in the situation was heavily tilted in my favor. It would be very easy for the perception—in safe-church-educated eyes—of abuse or inappropriateness to arise. I had to step carefully to avoid that.

Indeed, I had already done some careful tiptoeing. Earlier in the year, I took the students swimming in a friend's pool. It hadn't occurred to me that when you live in a shantytown, owning a bathing suit is not high on your list of priorities. The combination of clothing they found to swim in ranged from wildly to fantastically inappropriate and revealing. Persevering, however, I got in the pool and started helping one of the students inch her way into the deep end, her hands on my shoulders. As soon as she realized she could no longer touch the bottom, she screamed in terror and used my shoulders to push herself out of the water, in the process dragging her barely clad chest across my face. My "good touch, bad touch" training came rushing into my head and I realized I had done a very dumb thing. I told them to keep an eye on each other and removed myself from the swimming area for a while.

But I had so much hope for these students. That they had made it as far as high school was in some measure a testament to their talent and perseverance. I wanted only to remove obstacles from their lives so they could focus on their studies. It would be an abdication of my responsibility to avoid discussing something as important and fundamental to their lives as sex when it had the potential to create such great obstacles. It is precisely not talking about sex that has helped HIV become an epidemic in South Africa.

In the days following Luleka's test, I realized the message I wanted to communicate to these students was fairly simple—have an HIV test; if you have sex, use a condom; come to the clinic every twelve weeks for the birth control injection that will prevent pregnancy. The value I prized most was their education and I was concerned about sex insofar as it could create obstacles to that goal.

As I articulated these thoughts to myself, I realized that my true reluctance to start talking about sex with the students stemmed not from the language barrier—we were developing a common vocabulary; it would not be difficult to add a new subject—but from my fear of their reaction. What if I started talking about sex education and they rebelled? The rapport we had developed was the only thing allowing us to make the limited progress we had with *Charlie and the Chocolate Factory*. What if I jeopardized that by encouraging them to have an HIV test? And what could I really contribute? The students obviously had more experience with sex than me. I doubted my voice could add much authority or weight to their decisions.

I started small. While organizing some medical records, I happened to notice Ayabonga, one of the students, was overdue for her birth control shot. She already had one child, who was both delightful and an impediment to her education. At the end of the next class, while everyone else was talking with each other, I caught her eye and, doing my best to be as casual as possible, stammered, "Prevent," the English word women used to refer to birth control. To make sure Ayabonga understood, I made a stabbing motion in my thigh to indicate a shot. Though my discomfort with the situation was clear, she understood and shrugged: "When?"

"Yesterday," I responded.

She shrugged again, indicating she had forgotten and came into the clinic the next day. Clearly, they were all more comfortable with this than I was. Progress, I was coming to learn, would always come in very awkward and sporadic ways.

The conversation Vuyelwa and I began the day she told me about the attempted rape carried on over the next several months. She would occasionally ask to come along on my travels around town and I was happy to let her. Her motive for doing so was to convince me to help her open a hair salon, a business idea she had been nursing for some time but needed financing to help make a reality. I enjoyed the company when I was stuck in Mthatha's choking traffic and her experienced eyes pointed out aspects of life in Mthatha I missed. The relationship was an end in itself but occasionally, when the time was right, I tried to shift the conversation back to sex—asking about Bulumko, her son, who his father was, and whether she still knew him.

Vuyelwa's boyfriend and the father of her son was a young man named Phumlani. Though his family lived in Itipini, he spent most of his time in a rural village outside Mthatha, which meant they didn't get to spend much time together. But when they saw each other, they had sex and Phumlani didn't use a condom.

"Why not?" I asked her one day. Vuyelwa faithfully came into the clinic every twelve weeks for the birth control injection so she clearly didn't want to have another baby. "You need to use condoms to make sure you don't get any infections or HIV. Why don't you?"

"He says if I make him use a condom it means I don't love him or trust him," she replied. "He says you don't eat a sweet with the wrapper on."

"Well," I said, pleased to take advantage of an opportunity to empower women, "tell him, 'I am not a sweet. I am a young woman!'"

She laughed. I could tell that wasn't going to happen.

"Vuyelwa," I said. "It is important that you have only one . . ."

". . . boyfriend!" She cut me off, finishing the sentence. "I know. I only have one boyfriend. We trust each other."

"But you don't see him while he is away. You should use condoms. If you trust each other, you should both come to the clinic to be tested for HIV."

She laughed again. The thought of a healthy young man willingly coming into the clinic with his girlfriend for an HIV test was too unrealistic to be anything but humorous.

A few weeks later, soon after Sizeka had died, we were driving up to the Ngangalizwe health center to pick up some medicine. She had known Sizeka and knew I had been spending a lot of time with her, so she opened the conversation by asking, "How is Sizeka?"

"Vuyelwa, she died three days ago."

"Oh. I'm sorry." She stared out the window, clearly regretting having brought up the subject.

I wasn't sure how to do this in a way that respected the dead but I didn't want to let the teaching moment pass. "Vuyelwa, it is sad that Sizeka died but it shows why it is important to have an HIV test. If you are positive, then you can start getting the right pills earlier. Sizeka waited too long."

Vuyelwa seemed embarrassed to have brought up the topic of Sizeka but she was also scared to have known someone who died of HIV. On the drive back, Vuyelwa told me, "I will abstain. I am afraid of HIV."

It was a heartening thought but an unrealistic one, and I let her know that. "What will happen when Phumlani comes back the next time and wants to see you? What will you do then?"

"I will tell him I am abstaining."

"Really? What will he say to that?" She smiled uncomfortably back at me as she realized she might not be able to turn him down.

The conversation trailed off soon after that. It was too uncomfortable for me to take the topic further. What I wanted was for her to have an HIV test. I just didn't know how to talk about it.

Over the course of several months, we continued this on-again, off-again conversation but I eventually stopped pressing the matter. I had done everything I thought I possibly could and explained in as many ways possible the importance of having a test. But she continued to insist she was too afraid to find out. Talking about it anymore just smacked of desperation and prurience. It was easy for me to chalk it up as yet one more thing—along with getting a patient on ARVs, helping students pass school, and much more—that I just couldn't do.

My phone rang after work one day in late July. It was Vuyelwa. Phone conversations are necessarily short and succinct in Mthatha because few people can afford a lot of prepaid cell phone time. She said, "Jesse, today I went to a testing center and had a blood test. I am negative."

It was hard to know just how to respond. "That's great, Vuyelwa," I stammered. "I'm so happy you did that."

With that, she said goodbye and hung up.

I was shocked that she had had the test, at long last. I was overjoyed, of course, at her status. And I was moved that she wanted to make sure to tell me so soon after learning her results, to the extent that she called me rather than waiting until the next time we bumped into each other.

My time in Itipini was never not frustrating in some way. But it was encounters like Vuyelwa's phone call that nourished me and made me want to continue. Her test was the result of a relationship I had cultivated over many months. The phone call confirmed for me the importance of making such long-term commitments and showed me that relationships, even if they were ends in themselves, could still result in tangible benefits. Vuyelwa gave me credible reason to hope that my presence in Itipini had discernible positive impact.

Still, it was a sobering thought. After five months of conversation, I had succeeded in getting exactly one person to test for HIV. And there were scores more like her in Itipini, and millions more across the country and continent.

Ten

Get Up, Stand Up

PAKAMA CAME INTO THE clinic on the day Sizeka died, laboring up the three short steps to the door, pausing to support herself on the frame and catch her breath. She had recently tested positive for tuberculosis and was looking to start Directly Observed Therapy to cure the disease. Like many other people in her situation, she was HIV positive, weak, and barely able to walk on her own. As I organized her pills and took a look through her medical records, I realized she had recently started taking antiretroviral drugs. That was good news. Like Phatiswa, she had navigated the ARV system almost entirely on her own.

But I as flipped the pages of her tattered record book, I also noticed that she had recently been told to discontinue the ARVs. This was surprising. In order for ARVs to work, patients take them every day so the virus doesn't develop a resistance to the drugs. Indeed, ensuring the patients understand this is one of the main purposes of the preparatory process. Pakama had a date for another appointment at the Ngangalizwe health center and I knew she would be too weak to make it on her own. I offered her a lift so I could accompany her and learn more about the reasons behind this decision.

When the day arrived, I picked up Pakama and her mother Vivien from their shack. Vivien would have made a good Boy Scout—she was always prepared for everything. Since the lines could be lengthy and the waits never-ending, it was wise to bring along a little food, some juice, and one or two blankets, just in case things were so bad that they had to spend the night sleeping in line so they could be seen the next day.

On that first trip to Ngangalizwe with Pakama, I sought out Sister Nellie, the nurse in charge of the infectious diseases clinic that oversaw the ARV program. Nellie was a large woman; her clean, pressed uniform stretched across her stomach. Nurses in South Africa wear epaulets with pins that signify their level of training and areas of expertise. The shoulders of Nellie's uniform glinted with several shiny pieces of metal. She carried herself with a regal bearing, as befitted a nurse of her experience and stature. Nurses in South Africa command a great deal of respect and exert a tremendous amount of control over the health care system. In health centers like the one in Ngangalizwe, where the doctors, when they are around, are overwhelmed by patients, it is the nurses, and especially the most senior ones like Nellie, who wield all the power. When I first met her some months earlier, I was instantly intimidated.

I had been doing my best to speak as much Xhosa as possible with Nellie. Like many other people she seemed to appreciate my effort, even if I didn't always make sense. When the health center ran out of syringes or pills and asked if we had any to tide them over until the next shipment arrived, I would rush up with whatever they needed and make sure to personally deliver it into the hands of Nellie. My efforts at a closer relationship with her were slowly paying off. I slipped into Nellie's office between patients without earning too much enmity or wrath. Whether my presence was simply tolerated because of my skin color or genuinely appreciated because of my care for the patients I never knew. I suspected the former but I never bothered to ask.

Nellie told me that one of the drugs in the ARV regimen Pakama was taking was incompatible with the initial course of tuberculosis treatment. Pakama needed to carry on with the TB treatment and have the doctor write her a prescription for a different regimen. As Nellie was telling me this, I looked at the charts on the wall behind her, one of which listed the different government-provided ARV regimens. I could clearly see which regimen did not have the drug that conflicted with Pakama's TB treatment. I knew Nellie knew the ARV regimens backwards and forwards. It was obvious what needed to happen and we both knew it. "Sister Nellie," I said. "Can't you just switch her to regimen 1b right now?"

Sister Nellie looked at me like the idea was ludicrous. "A doctor has to write a prescription for the new regimen." It was a law-like statement. I knew from past experience that no amount of arguing, cajoling, or pleading would get me anywhere. I let the discussion drop. Nellie referred Pakama to the doctor to change the regimen but also noted that Pakama was complaining of constipation and general abdominal distress. These, no doubt, were symptoms of her failing immune system. The key was to get Pakama back on ARVs.

When I went to get Pakama two days later for the appointment with the doctor, her condition had deteriorated yet further. She was sleeping in her bed in her shack, under a giant pile of old and worn blankets. It was June, the beginning of winter, and it could be quite cool at night but not in the middle of the morning with the sun shining under a clear blue sky. I asked how she was and all she could say was, "I'm cold." She labored even to say that. It took her ages to get out of bed, wash her face, and leave her shack. When she did, she was supported by Vivien and a neighbor, who helped her into my car. I dropped them off at the health center and they joined a long line of patients.

When I returned in the early afternoon, Pakama and Vivien were waiting outside for me. I eagerly checked her card, expecting to see a new prescription, but all I saw was a list of the symptoms of her abdominal pain and a prescription for some vitamins we could have given her in the clinic. The doctor also suggested that she get an ultrasound of her abdomen to exclude the possibility that her TB had spread. It seemed slightly absurd—after all, Pakama had never had TB before, and she had been diagnosed so recently that it was virtually impossible the TB could have spread so quickly from her lungs. Sister Nellie happened to be walking by and I showed her the card. "How come she didn't get a new regimen?" I asked brusquely, my tone reflecting the frustration I was feeling.

Nellie's face flickered at the impertinence of my question as she glanced at the card. "The doctor says she needs an ultrasound to exclude TB abdomen," she said, pointing to the card as if it were obvious. It was again said in a tone I recognized, one that could explain the way things were but not explain why they were not as they should be. I thanked her and we returned to Itipini. The next available ultrasound appointment wasn't for three and a half weeks but Pakama's health was continuing to deteriorate. She could no longer walk to the clinic for her TB treatment so I brought her the pills in her shack each day.

Despite the absence of any progress, Pakama maintained a steady inner core of confidence. She had a simple and overwhelming desire to stay alive. She was eager to work past her health problems and move on with her life, independent from what we could offer her in the clinic. Pakama's directness and forthrightness contrasted sharply with the despair and hopelessness I had seen Sizeka endure as she died. When I visited Pakama with her TB pills, she was not shy about letting me know what was hurting or how weak she felt. Though I needed no reminding, she made sure I knew when we had to go back for another appointment. While many other patients deferred to my guidance—even when I was ill-equipped to provide it—Pakama knew how the system worked at the health center and directed me accordingly.

This determination occasionally spilled over into a quite demanding attitude. Once, when I went to check on them waiting in line at Ngangalizwe, Pakama told me, "I'm cold. I want a blanket." It was a warm day and Vivien had evidently not thought blankets would be necessary. Pakama was insistent, however, so when I returned a little later I brought with me a spare blanket. Despite her gaunt face and generalized weakness, Pakama confidently sat up in the wheelchair I had found for her and deigned to receive the blanket from my hand. As she arranged it around her, the line inched forward. "Quba, mama," she said and pointed forward, using the imperative form of the all-purpose Xhosa word for "drive" or "move forward." Vivien obliged and pushed her wheelchair a little farther ahead. In other situations in Itipini, I was having trouble handling demanding people. With Pakama I was delighted to see a patient who was so invested in her health. That inner determination was the critical factor in those lengthy weeks when we attempted to correct her ARV prescription.

The word *pakama* in Xhosa means "get up" or "stand up," and I couldn't help thinking about Jesus' command to the paralytic in the Gospel of Matthew: "stand up, take your bed, and go home." It was what I wanted more than anything for Pakama, to see her stand up from her wheelchair and go to her home. Jesus had it easy, commanding the man to walk and seeing it happen. Pakama was trying to stand up but the obstacles were substantial. I worried she would run out of time before her prescription could be fixed.

Nonetheless—and undeterred by the experience with Sizeka—I began to let myself hope that Pakama would be my success story, the one I could point out to future visitors as one whose life had been changed by ARVs. Sizeka hadn't made it, but Pakama, I hoped, could. Still, it seemed like a long journey and she was getting sicker by the day.

ᕮᖅ

Aside from Vivien, Pakama shared the family's shack with Fezile, her younger brother. He was a thin man with a gigantic smile. When I made my house calls with TB medications, he greeted me warmly, grinning broadly and calling me "Mr. Jesses." We talked about the weather, often the only non-health-related topic I could discuss in Xhosa. Occasionally, I saw him in town, pushing around a cart with the other men, looking for work. A few shacks away, down the hill closer to the river, lived Vivien's sister, Sylvia. A short and compact older woman, she could have been Vivien's twin. Sylvia had her own family, with a son and a daughter close in age to their cousins, Pakama and Fezile. Her children had other homes, however, and weren't often around Itipini. I heard reference to the son, Siyambonga, but he was a mystery to me.

Fezile and Sylvia were both HIV positive. This was not a surprise to learn. A man as thin as Fezile clearly had some health issues. HIV was a logical explanation. Like Pakama, Fezile had recently started on ARVs. That he could work in town was a good indication, I thought, that his strength was increasing. While I was happy to chat with him, it was easy to relegate him to the margins of my thoughts. Too many HIV patients, like Pakama, couldn't even walk. All I could do for Fezile was remind him to keep taking his ARVs—he needed no reminder—and hope for the best.

Fezile's condition took a modest-seeming turn for the worse when he showed up in the clinic one day, looking dehydrated. He had been vomiting and suffering diarrhea for a day or two. It was a familiar complaint for AIDS patients. Dorothy took it seriously, giving him rehydration solution and referring him to Ngangalizwe for further treatment. I was heading into town and offered him a ride but he assured me with a big smile that he could make it on his own.

Even as I hoped for the best for her, throughout the weeks of near-daily visits with Pakama, I had been mentally preparing myself for the morning when we pulled into Itipini and learned that she had died. The shock I had felt when Sizeka died was still fresh in my mind and I didn't want to be surprised again. Pakama's deteriorating condition forced me to acknowledge that death was firmly in the realm of possible outcomes, no matter how many appointments I drove her to.

It was with a sinking heart, then, that a few mornings after Fezile's visit to the clinic, I arrived for work to see a mournful Vivien. Pakama is dead, I thought to myself. To our shock, though, Vivien had come to inform us of Fezile's death. He had made it to the Ngangalizwe health center but it wasn't enough. The AIDS had overwhelmed his ARVs. Just like that, he was gone.

The family spent the week following his death in mourning in the shack, preparing for the funeral. But it was also the week of Pakama's ultrasound appointment. It was a rainy winter morning, cold and dreary, when I went to check on Pakama to make sure she was ready. There was a small fire burning in the center of the shack. Rain dripped in through holes in the roof and walls. Pakama was sitting in bed, struggling to gather the energy to prepare for her appointment. There were two pots placed on the bed to catch the rainwater and the blanket was damp. It was no wonder, I thought, that she was cold, if this was the only refuge she had from the weather.

While Pakama got herself ready, I did my best to join the mourning family members around the sputtering fire and pay my condolences. All I could think to talk about was how much I had appreciated Fezile's cheery attitude and smile. It wasn't clear how well my fractured Xhosa was understood but I hoped my demeanor was. I knew that when you visited a mourning family it was proper to stay, eat, and pray a while. I didn't have the time. I was happy to pay my condolences but I also wanted to be sure that Pakama didn't miss the appointment for which we had been waiting so long. After a few short minutes, we were off.

To this point, Sylvia, Pakama's aunt, had been a mostly tangential presence in my interactions with the family. But shortly after Fezile's funeral, a neighbor asked me to visit Sylvia and see how she was. I found her curled in a ball on her bed, looking gaunt and weak, complaining, as Pakama often did, about the cold. When I checked her records, I learned she hadn't had a CD4 count in years. It was frustrating to me that while one half of the family could keep up with the demands of HIV-related care, the other half, living only a stone's throw away, couldn't. Had it ever occurred to Vivien to suggest that her sister do what Pakama and Fezile had successfully managed to do and start taking ARVs? But that was all past. I offered a resigned sigh and helped Sylvia to the clinic. Jenny drew her blood and sent it off to the lab. We would have to wait at least a week to learn if she was eligible to start ARVs.

While we waited, Sylvia's daughter, who happened to be in Itipini at the time, was insistent that her mother be allowed to go back to her rural village. This confused me. ARVs were most easily accessible in Mthatha. If the family went home, I explained, it would be much harder to go through the preparation process. But the daughter wouldn't listen to me. I couldn't blame her. One cousin on the much-vaunted ARVs, Fezile, had died, and it seemed likely that another, Pakama, would soon join him. I also knew that older people, when they got very sick, summoned all their energy and insisted on returning to their home village, in order to die at "home" regardless of how long they had lived in Itipini.

Sylvia's CD4 results, when they came back, were predictably low enough to begin preparation for the ARVs. But when the family went to Ngangalizwe, Sister Nellie, at their request, referred Sylvia to the clinic closest to their village. The family began making plans in earnest to take Sylvia home. I wanted to intervene and prevent them from leaving. The medical care in Mthatha was a long way from perfect (or even good) but it was still the best in the region. Staying in Itipini offered Sylvia the best chance of surviving. But Sylvia, it was clear, had given up hope of surviving and wanted to die at home. I stood by, silently fuming, as they made plans. They were giving up too early. Death for me was too final, too much the end.

Even in the few days it took to make arrangements for the trip, Sylvia's health declined dramatically. She moved into Pakama's shack so Vivien could care for both of them at once. Sylvia lay on a mattress near the fire where only a week or so earlier the family had been mourning Fezile's death. On my first visit after Vivien had moved in, I didn't immediately recognize her. She was losing weight so dramatically that her appearance was changing.

In the midst of all this—mourning for one family member with a dying relative on the floor of the shack—Pakama had yet another doctor's appointment. As I headed to the shack that morning, I passed an unfamiliar *bakkie* parked on the road. The door to the shack, usually open, was closed. I was so familiar with the family at this point that I knocked and entered without waiting for a reply, shouting a greeting as I did so. The shack was full of family members and neighbors and there was one man in the center, showing some forms and talking. I couldn't catch his Xhosa but it was clear he was explaining what each form was for.

Everyone turned at my interruption, with a collective look that said I should have known better than to barge in at this moment. From across the room, I looked closer at the forms and recognized them as death certificates. The pieces began to fall into place. The *bakkie* outside was a hearse. The man in the center was from the funeral home. He was explaining to the family how the death had to be reported to the Department of Home Affairs. But who had died? Not Pakama, please. I looked quickly around the room. Pakama was staring back at me. Sylvia had died.

The awkwardness of the circumstances overwhelmed whatever grief I felt. I had barged in on the family, unaware they were dealing with yet another death. It would have been difficult to know how to react appropriately to the situation in English; navigating it in Xhosa proved too much. Aware that my face was burning with embarrassment, I mouthed the word "doctor" to Pakama, offered my condolences as best and as briefly as I could, and backed my way out of the door as quickly as possible, saying I'd come back later.

Not long after Sylvia died, her son Siyambonga briefly entered the picture. He had been living and working elsewhere so it had been twelve years since his last visit to our clinic. He was a familiar sight when he was carried in: gaunt, emaciated, and wasting away. Lying there on the stretcher on the floor of the clinic, he looked overwhelmed and confused, clearly not understanding what was going on, and despairing of his future. I took him to the hospital and they were able to care a little for his symptoms, while we waited for his CD4 count results. But it was all far too little, far too late. He died less than a week after he first returned to the clinic.

In the span of a few months, three of Pakama's relations had died from the very same virus that was causing her so much trouble. At one point, Jenny and I were tracking so many patients with the same last name from the same family that we couldn't keep all their names straight. Who's whose mother here? How are they related again? If it was so overwhelming for us, how must it have seemed to Pakama? That she kept her fierce desire to live in the face of a steady drumbeat of death was all the more remarkable.

When it finally happened, the ultrasound, predictably, didn't reveal anything unusual. The laxative prescribed by one doctor for the abdominal distress wasn't helping. We were stuck. Pakama needed a new ARV regimen, and the system that was designed to care for her was failing to produce it. Having been passed from doctor to doctor—as the system mandated—she seemed in danger of slipping through the cracks.

It was a situation that made me question my own role as a missionary. Up to that point, I had seen accompanying patients as an important part of my work. It was an obvious need and a way for me to be present with patients at a difficult time in their life and help direct them to the care they needed. There had been instances in the past in which the fact that I had transported a patient had mattered a great deal and significantly contributed to their improvement. But Pakama's weeks-long saga made me confront the reality that just getting someone into the health care system—the goal of all my trips—did not guarantee them the care they needed. For that, the system itself needed to function properly. Clearly, a system that knew what pills Pakama required but could not immediately produce a prescription for them, despite repeated attempts over several weeks, was not functioning as it needed to.

The idea of incarnational ministry still motivated me, and I continued to try to become a part of the way of life in Itipini and Mthatha as best I could. My ultimate goal, of course, was to help people make improvements, but those changes would only come from the relationships that grew out of my decision to share an existence with people in Itipini. This is part of the reason I became friendly with and worked towards relationships with nurses like Nellie; they helped grease important wheels and made life and health improvements easier to realize.

But the relationships didn't eliminate my frustration with the inefficiencies of the health care system. Throughout my time with Pakama, I toyed with the idea of visiting the doctor with her. If I had spent the hours waiting with Pakama and Vivien, I could have explained the entire situation to the doctor and, with luck, prevailed upon him to write the necessary new prescription. But there were always other patients to tend to while Pakama waited, and the idea went against my conception of my position. I needed to get Pakama into the health care system. Once

I had done so I needed to trust the system would take care of her. Yet it clearly wasn't.

In a situation like Pakama's, I wondered if my simultaneous desires to change her condition and be in relationship with the nurses might not be at odds. How could I change the system when I had become a part of it? If I pressed too hard in Pakama's favor, I worried the nurses might take my implicit criticism of the system as criticism of their work. If I spent all my energy trying to work the system for this one patient, I doubted I would have enough energy left over to be present—and being present, I was learning, required lots of energy—with the scores of others in Itipini. Even if I did change the system for one patient, I did not want to create the expectation that I would do the same for others, further drawing my focus away from the simple act of being present. The success of "front lines" missionaries like myself depended on our presence. Could we also be the people who worked towards the systemic change that was obviously necessary? Or were activism and presence implacably at odds?

In Pakama's case, there was a middle way, and it was the one I chose. Frustrated at not getting anywhere after repeated appointments, I took all her paperwork and went to see Sister Nellie. I explained Pakama's continuing decline and asked what could be done about it. Sister Nellie could, I am sure, detect my barely concealed aggravation and had noticed Pakama's decline herself. Whatever it was that convinced her, she told me to bring Pakama back the next day and she would sort out the matter with the doctor.

As I settled Pakama in her wheelchair the next morning, I noticed she was looking much weaker than normal and didn't seem like her usual forthright and direct self. She had been living so close to the edge for so long. I wondered if she would have the strength to come back to health if she was able to get the ARVs. I was trusting in Nellie's promise and hoping this would be the last appointment in this seemingly never-ending go-around in the health care system.

Vivien and Pakama had to wait quite a while that day but it was worth it. When I picked them up, I immediately snatched the card out of Pakama's hand. There, in a barely legible script, above a stamp from a doctor, I read, "switch to regimen 1b." When their turn had come, Sister Nellie went in with them and explained the situation to the doctor. He happily obliged, trusting in Nellie's accumulated knowledge and the obvious facts of the situation. It was the same regimen Sister Nellie and I realized Pakama needed by looking at the poster weeks earlier. It was the regimen that Sister Nellie knew all along was needed. But it was only now that a doctor had written it that it was legitimate.

We picked up the ARVs from the pharmacy that day and Pakama took them as soon as we returned to her shack. I went to see her a few hours later to provide her TB treatment, expecting to find her, as always, lying in her bed, complaining about the cold. To my surprise, she was sitting up, near the cooking area of the shack, and having her hair done by a friend. And she was her usual independent self again, barely looking at me and telling me to leave the pills on the shelf by the door so she could take them later. I smiled and obliged. It was amazing how quickly the pills had changed her health.

Much of that initial improvement was illusory, however. Pakama's health had significantly deteriorated and it was a long climb back. I had to continue to make house visits for her to give her her TB pills. She was getting stronger but still spent a lot of time in bed. One surprising indication that she was getting better came on a visit not long afterwards. I heard a deep voice coming from around the corner where Pakama's bed was. Not thinking quickly enough, I poked my head around the corner to give Pakama her pills, and I found her lying in bed with a man I had never seen before. They weren't in any compromising positions and appeared to have most of their clothes on. But I didn't stay long enough to investigate the matter further. I smiled awkwardly, greeted them, dropped the pills off, and left, relieved she might at last have some surplus energy.

(Later, I learned the man was Pakama's long-term boyfriend. Like many male partners, he disappeared when Pakama became so sick because she had been unable to cook and clean for him. His reappearance on the scene was truly an indicator of Pakama's improving health. It meant he thought she would make it and he didn't need to find another woman in his life.)

A few days later, I was aimlessly working in the clinic and happened to glance towards the door. I was shocked to see Pakama sitting quietly on a stool, modestly out of breath from the walk to the clinic and leaning on a walking stick, but there nonetheless. For the first time in all the weeks and months I had known her she had made it into the clinic on her own and wanted to take her tuberculosis medication in the clinic. To see her sitting there, aided only by a stick and accompanied by no one, gave me a feeling of unequaled satisfaction. It had been a lot of work and frustration but we—I—had contributed directly to reversing the decline of a patient's health. The feeling was tempered by the knowledge that Pakama was still quite sick. But she was moving in the right direction and I could draw hope from that.

Over the next several weeks Pakama's health continued to improve modestly. I saw less and less of her, as there were fewer reasons to visit her shack and fewer appointments to drive her to. She kept coming into the clinic for her TB treatment but I wasn't always around, often off with the next sick patient, repeating the same trip through clinics and hospitals in search of desperately needed care. Not long afterward, I left Mthatha for a few weeks, confident of Pakama's improving condition.

One of the first places I visited on my first day back was Pakama's shack. Vivien smiled to see me after my absence, and when we had greeted each other, I asked where Pakama was.

"She doesn't live here anymore."

"Where does she live?" I asked, worried something had happened.

"Over there," she said, with a wave of her hand up the hill.

"Can she walk on her own?" I wanted to know.

"Oh, yes, very well," she replied, and a big smile came over her face.

I set off in the direction Vivien had indicated and—using my usual strategy for finding people when I didn't know where they lived—shouted her name.

Eventually I heard a disinterested "What?" in response from a nearby shack.

"Pakama," I said. "It's Jesse."

I poked my head in the shack and saw her washing clothes. She smiled broadly to see me again and asked how I was.

"I'm fine," I said. "But I want to know how you are. Can you walk?"

"Yes," she replied but with a hint of embarrassment. I was a reminder of her recent, sicker life and it was clear she didn't want to relive those weeks spent complaining of the cold in her bed.

She was clearly supporting herself just fine while washing the clothes but I needed to see for myself. "Show me," I said.

Now she was really embarrassed. I knew I was making too big a deal out of her and it was difficult for her to recall her illness. She gave me a look that said, "What do you think? Of course I can walk by myself." But there was no one else around so she obliged and stepped outside. Without struggle or undue effort, she casually walked down one side of the shack and back to the door and then turned to look to see if I was satisfied. I was. She was like a whole new person.

Friends at home often asked me if I thought there was any hope in the face of the AIDS epidemic. Seeing Pakama walk confirmed there was. The drugs exist to minimize the effects of HIV and reverse the progress of AIDS. The challenge in Itipini is getting them into the hands of the right people before it is too late. In Pakama's case, we succeeded, but only just.

More than giving me hope in the face of the epidemic, seeing Pakama walk that day gave me hope for my own role in Itipini. After endlessly frustrating months of feeling like I wasn't actually able to do anything, of repeatedly running into barriers of language, culture, and race, I saw in Pakama a clear example of a person in whose life my efforts had made a difference. It had taken time—countless car rides, hospital trips, and visits to her shack—and neither of us had been entirely sure how to get what we needed. But the results were best seen in the steps Pakama had taken on her own: on that first day when she walked into the clinic unaided and on that day when I saw her sashay across her front yard.

I had struck a blow against a giant epidemic. I had helped—saved, even—someone. I had *done* something.

Eleven

The Loan Shark

THE SUCCESS I WAS having with people like Pakama and Vuyelwa showed me that I could—at last!—have a discernibly positive impact on people's lives. Perhaps saving people wasn't too far-fetched of an idea after all. It had just taken some time to figure out how. Buoyed, I kept looking for ways to broaden my role in Itipini. There were plenty of people who weren't on the verge of death but still needed help.

These were the people who occupied my thinking as winter took hold. The early mornings in June and July were frigid. I had to warm up the car for five minutes before it would shift into gear without stalling and remind myself that I was, in fact, still in Africa. A young woman I knew named Yoliswa had recently moved out of Itipini and into a neighborhood named after liberation hero Chris Hani that I drove past every day. Because of the cooler weather she started calling and asking for a ride into town so she wouldn't have to wait for a taxi in the cold.

Yoliswa and I had met several months earlier in the kitchen in Itipini. It had been a quiet day in the clinic and I had wandered over to see if there were any leftovers. I had seen Yoliswa around in those first months but she had been just one more face in the sea of humanity I encountered each day. On this day, she was in the kitchen helping serve lunch. As she handed me a plate of leftovers, she said something in rapid Xhosa I didn't understand.

"What was that?" I asked Ncediwe, the preschool teacher who was standing at the door.

"She says she wants to marry you because then she can cook for you every day," Ncediwe said. Yoliswa smiled shyly. I knew she had understood my question and Ncediwe's reply. The food the women cooked for lunch was fine, but the thought of having it every day for the rest of my life was enough to put me off the idea of marriage altogether.

The other conversations in the kitchen had stopped and all eyes were fixed on me, waiting for my reply. I stammered out the first thing that came to mind: "I'm too young." The women scoffed. Girls eight or ten years younger than me were giving birth in Itipini. I was more than old enough to have married and fathered several children. Even I knew this to be true, given the number of friends of mine who were getting married back home.

I wanted to say something like "I'm not ready yet" but I couldn't figure out how to communicate the thought in Xhosa. Nor did I think the idea of being "ready" for marriage would translate. Relationships and marriage were something that just happened to people in Itipini, whether or not they were prepared. I tried next to say that I didn't love Yoliswa, but the word for like and love in Xhosa is the same and I didn't know how to communicate that I wasn't in love with her—I didn't even really know her—without offending her. Nor did it seem like love was truly a criterion for some of the relationships I had seen. I thought I could say I didn't have enough money to be married but I knew that wouldn't work. They would just laugh and laugh and wish they had my income.

I was flailing around for an acceptable answer when my friend Noxolo looked over at me and said, "Say you don't have the *lobola*," the price paid in cows by the groom to the bride's family. She had hit upon the solution. "I don't have the *lobola*," I said. "I don't have any cows." The onlooking women dissolved in laughter, Yoliswa smiled with a twinge of disappointment, and the moment passed.

But I couldn't forget Yoliswa after that and began to recognize her more frequently around Itipini. She was twenty-one, HIV positive, and had three children, ranging in age from about ten months to six years. Her positive HIV test had come many years before, but her CD4 count was high and she was thoroughly asymptomatic. She had dropped out of school when she had her first child and in the intervening years had not been able to find work, surviving instead on government grants. Despite the circumstances, she had a bubbly and effervescent personality virtually every time I saw her. She was one of the first older people to take advantage of the library I was just then creating with Mkuseli. Her favorite books were the ones with Disney characters, and when she returned one to me I asked her what it had been about. She paused and looked embarrassed and then did a fine job summarizing the plot in English.

It came as a surprise one day to be told that Yoliswa had moved out of Itipini and was living in Chris Hani. Her aunt had invited her to live with her and Yoliswa had accepted to get her three children out of Itipini. The trouble was that like many of the other new neighborhoods that have sprung up in Mthatha's breakneck growth, Chris Hani has almost no basic services. Yoliswa returned to the clinic from time to time for CD4 counts or when her children were sick. I didn't want to become her private taxi but she knew I drove past every day. When she called, it wasn't hard to pick her up and I enjoyed having the company on the morning commute. Driving into town on that wintry morning in June, I noticed that Bongamusa, her middle child, had some impressive-looking warm clothes. "They look new," I said. "Where did you get them?"

"At Pep," she said, naming a popular and inexpensive clothing store. "But they are too expensive. The children need clothes because it is cold but the clothes take all the money I get from the grants. It is still the beginning of the month but all my grants are gone. How do you buy clothes and food as well?"

I responded with a murmur of sympathy, preparing myself for the inevitable request for money. But Yoliswa spared me the need to say anything by continuing on.

"I want to get a job, Jesse."

Everyone wanted a job. The unemployment rate was staggering and there just weren't enough jobs for everyone to have one. "I know, Yoliswa," I sighed. "What do you want to do?"

"Anything. I want to make money for my children."

Jenny and I had just begun discussing the idea of a small micro-credit program in Itipini. The idea is common in development circles and is based on the premise that what poor people lack is not knowledge or skills but access to credit. If you give people—primarily women—the capital they need to start a business, they can earn enough money to pay back the initial loan and generate income for themselves. Spurred on by a former volunteer, Jenny and I were thinking about how it might apply to our work in Itipini and we wanted a test case to begin with. Yoliswa no longer lived in Itipini but she seemed as good a candidate as any to try the idea on.

"Yoliswa," I said, tentatively broaching the subject. "There are lots of women who work in town selling things, like clothes or fruit or sweets. Lots of people make jobs for themselves. Is there anything like that you've ever been interested in?" Glancing at her, I could tell the idea had sparked some interest. "If you had an idea, we could talk about how you might be able to get started."

"Let me think about it," she said. We had almost arrived in Itipini.

The next week Yoliswa called me and in her usual bright tone of voice told me she had a business idea. But her tone dropped almost immediately, and in the next breath she said dejectedly, "It is too much money." I knew from experience that my idea of "too much money" and Yoliswa's would likely be different so I told her we would talk about it some more.

I stopped by Yoliswa's house that afternoon on the way back from Itipini. Her new home was made out of the same corrugated tin that characterized so many homes in Itipini with the critical difference that Chris Hani was not built on a garbage dump. In fact, because it was newer, Chris Hani was a fairly spacious place, with plenty of room between the houses and a stunning view over the mountains to the north. The inside consisted of a single cramped but pleasant room with just enough space for two double beds and a cooking area. It was home for Yoliswa, her aunt, and the six children they cared for between them.

Dinner was being prepared and the room was cramped so we stepped outside to hear each other speak. "Jesse," she said excitedly. "I want to sell clothes." It was not an uncommon idea. Women traveled to larger cities a few hours away, bought clothes in bulk from wholesalers, and sold them on the street in Mthatha. Yoliswa, however, had another market in mind. "I want to sell here," she said, sweeping her hand around to encompass all of Chris Hani and the neighboring area, Mandela Park. "Only three other women sell clothes here and I can walk around to the houses and sell things like winter coats and shoes."

She had researched the logistics—where she would buy the clothes, where her children would go while she was working, and so forth—and had good answers to all the questions I asked. Eventually, I got around to the question I knew she was waiting for me to ask. "How much money do you need to begin?"

"It is too much," she said again and looked away.

"How much?" I asked.

"One point five," she said, looking at me with a new bit of hope in her eyes. That meant fifteen hundred rand, at the time a little less than two hundred US dollars and well within the range of what Jenny and I had set as the maximum loan we would consider. She needed about 150 rand for the taxi fare to and from the town where she would buy the clothes, 150 rand for day care for her children, and the rest for stocking clothes.

"Yoliswa, that's fine. That is not too much money," I said.

"Really?" Her eyes lit up and her face regained its usual cheer.

We discussed a repayment plan. I didn't want the loan to drag on forever but I also wanted her to be realistic about how much she could afford to pay me. She suggested the idea of 150 rand per month. When she explained her reasoning, it seemed to make sense.

"Let me think about it and I'll call you again so we can talk about it some more."

Yoliswa didn't wait for me to call her. She called a few days later and said only, "*Well*?" in a long, drawn-out, expectant sort of way. I agreed to stop by later that afternoon.

The truth was that I was proceeding blindly with the idea. I wasn't a business expert but I thought I knew enough basic questions—where's the market? what are the costs? what's the revenue?—to make a credible attempt at it. More than that, I felt I knew Yoliswa well enough to trust that the research she had done was correct and that she was as committed to the idea as she seemed to be. She appeared to have a realistic understanding of what it would take and how hard she would have to work. It was clear that she understood that the money was not a gift but a loan and she would have to pay it back over time.

I wanted to draw in another person to support Yoliswa so she wouldn't be entirely on her own. That afternoon when I arrived at Yoliswa's home, I asked Yoliswa's aunt to come outside with me. The sun was setting over the hills and it was a gorgeous—and chilly—evening.

"Has Yoliswa told you what we've been talking about?" I asked.

"Yes," she responded. "You are helping her a lot."

"This isn't an easy thing. It means Yoliswa has to get up every day and work, to take a taxi all the way to Queenstown, to bring the clothes back, and to walk all around here to try to sell them."

"I know."

"It is a lot of money and Yoliswa has to repay it. Do you think that will be a problem?"

She shook her head.

"Is it alright if Yoliswa stores those clothes in the house until she sells them?"

"Oh, yes."

"Will you be able to encourage her and support her?" I felt like I was working my way through the baptismal covenant.

She gave me a look that said, "Of course." What she actually said was, "Yoliswa knows that I am always there to help her."

I left, promising to think about it further and call Yoliswa in a few days.

I couldn't think of many more hoops I wanted Yoliswa to jump through, and she seemed like a good test case for the larger program we were hoping to start in Itipini. I visited Yoliswa once more to review the details of the idea and she was clearly anxious for a final decision from me. On the car ride home, I decided there was no reason I shouldn't lend the money to Yoliswa. All I had to lose was the cash.

On a Saturday morning a week later, I stopped by Yoliswa's house with the money stuffed in an envelope in my pocket. I called her outside and told her to count the bills. Her eyes were wide as she did so but it was all there. "Put it in a safe place until Monday," I said. She stuffed it in her bra, the place where most South African women keep their valuables.

I could tell she was overwhelmed by the moment and she didn't have much to say. She just opened her arms, gave me a big smile, and said, "May I?" We sealed the loan with a hug in her front yard.

On Monday, she called to say that she'd been to Queenstown and purchased all the clothes she could afford. I went over after work to check out the purchases. A modest but impressive array of sweaters, shirts, and shoes were laid out on the bed and there was already one woman looking them over. They were the kind of things I had seen other people wearing in town, which gave me confidence they would sell. Yoliswa was more excited than I had ever seen her. "Jesse, I want to start a big business and sell lots of clothes. I want to go to Durban and buy clothes there. They are more classy there. I want to support all my children." It was hard not to get caught up in her enthusiasm. I thought about how I was going to tell my supporters back home about her and point to her as an example of what can happen when we are incarnate in different cultures, learn how things work, and build relationships with people. But I didn't let Yoliswa see my excitement. Instead, I soberly reminded her of the importance of starting small. We would go through a few months with clothes from Queenstown before we thought about making things any larger.

There was nothing I could do but wait. Poor people would not get rich overnight, no matter how hard I tried. It would always be a long and arduous process. When I returned in three weeks, the date of our first scheduled repayment, Yoliswa rushed excitedly out of the house and with a smile on her face handed me 150 rand. As much as I had hoped for this moment, I was still a bit stunned that everything had worked as planned. Yoliswa had been back to Queenstown to restock and was on her second round of clothing. Our visit that day was short. There didn't seem like anything I could do except let her keep working.

Two things convinced Jenny and me it was worth trying to expand the microcredit idea to Itipini at large. The first was Yoliswa's initial success. The second was the newest addition to our staff, a recent college graduate named Unathi, who was in an experimental social worker position. She had a lifetime of knowledge about what worked in Mthatha and what didn't. Ideally, she would eventually be able to step into the administrative role and keep the program running without my assistance; to be successful, it had to be able to expand and grow independent of my presence.

I was hopeful as well that the program would help me deal with a daily frustration in Itipini. From the drunk men outside the *shebeens* asking for a few rand, to the mothers asking for help buying uniforms, to the patients I dropped off at the hospital wanting money for food, I was perpetually being asked for money, creating tests of my situational ethics that I sometimes passed but more often failed. Saying no to a drunk man was easy, but I was learning to be as suspicious of mothers asking for money for school in the middle of the school year, long after the bills were due. Money was something I had that people in Itipini needed and I was happy to help how I could. But I also knew that money could corrode the very relationships that were so central to what I saw as my work there. The microcredit program, I thought, would be a way to help people generate more money for themselves, rather than continually turning to me or Jenny or whomever.

Unathi and I launched the program not long after Yoliswa's first repayment. Standing in front of about eighty women after our morning prayers, I explained how the program would work. I had learned the Xhosa word for "to lend" for this very purpose and emphasized it repeatedly. If borrowers repaid their loans, we would be able to relend the money to future borrowers, cycling it through the community to the benefit of as many as possible. The women responded positively and in the next two weeks, more than a dozen business proposals trickled in. They were written on spare scraps of paper—a name, an idea, and a basic outline of how much it would cost.

In the meantime, I was reading about microcredit programs and designing something that would work in Itipini. The borrowers had to be prepared for the idea of working at their business every day and committed to the idea of repaying. Before they received any money, I wanted them to overcome hurdles I set up to test their seriousness. I wanted them to do further research on their ideas and attend a series of interviews and classes with Unathi and me. And I didn't want to lend the money to borrowers in isolation. Microcredit programs are traditionally centered on group-based borrowing, in which an entire group of women takes part in the preparation for borrowing but only one is lent money. In Itipini, we knew all the prospective borrowers from their frequent trips to the clinic, their children in the preschool, and their regular presence around the Community Project area. Instead of groups, we required that each prospective borrower have a business support partner who could come to all the meetings, learn the same basic information, and be responsible for encouraging the borrower to make repayments. The combination of the supporter and our preexisting network of relationships seemed a sufficient replacement for the group-based approach. Moreover, word of our program was spreading quickly and we had a growing waiting list. The women on the waiting list knew they wouldn't be lent any money until the first group began to make repayments. I hoped that social pressure would have a positive impact on the first borrowers.

It was an exciting time as Unathi and I set about interviewing candidates. There was a range of ideas: one woman was interested in selling fruits and sweets at the school during the break the students had, another already made and sold dresses and wanted a loan to expand the business, and several young women wanted to sell cell phone airtime in town. The major cell carriers sold pay-as-you-go airtime in bulk at a discount so people could sell it at face value and keep the difference as profit. Two other women were interested in starting spaza shops, the little shops that sold staple goods, in their homes. Another young woman wanted to sell chickens, bought wholesale at a farm outside of town.

The prospective borrowers were excited about their ideas and eager to get the money. But they also seemed to have an inflated fear of debt and pitched small ideas that failed to take account of the economies of scale that could come from a larger initial loan. They proposed unreasonably rapid repayment plans that relied on inflated profit projections to pay off the loan within a few, short months. Unathi and I stressed the ways debt could be an ally and said repayment was not something to be worried about, so long as the business was running smoothly. We sent them away from each individual meeting with a homework assignment, mostly to do more research on the particular costs involved in their idea.

The interview process, stretching over several weeks, also eliminated unserious borrowers. One prospective borrower and her supporter showed up to a meeting drunk and incapable of speaking coherently. We politely asked them to leave and crossed them off the list. Another older woman could not understand the difference between the capital she needed to keep the business going and the profit she could spend for herself. Unathi had an impressive business acumen and tried repeatedly to explain it to her, but it was obvious from the borrower's questions and the look on her face that she did not understand at all. She was an older woman and had only made it to second grade in the old Transkei school system so it was no surprise that her math was limited. I regretted crossing her off the list, but we had limited funds and the younger borrowers had a better grasp of what was expected of them.

The plans the borrowers presented weren't just business plans. Several had young children. If they were too young for the preschool, where would they be while their mother was in town working? In each case, we settled on what seemed to be an acceptable solution, often a grandmother or neighbor who would be around to provide child care. There were other delicate issues to address as well. I knew all the candidates from the clinic and I knew a majority of them were HIV positive. But it didn't seem like that was a reason to disqualify them. After

Pakama, I was busy preaching to anyone who would listen about the hope and help that existed for people with HIV.

The centerpiece of our preparation was a series of classes in business principles that Unathi and I offered to our borrowers and their supporters. Admittedly, I had been a classics and not an economics major in university, but that didn't deter me. Twenty-five women crammed into the small shipping container we used for the English classes. On this day, what I wanted to communicate was the importance of always setting aside enough capital to continue the business. Nozandile, the young woman who wanted to sell chickens, was my example.

"If Nozandile buys ten chickens at forty rand each, how much will that cost her?" I asked.

They could do the math: "Four hundred rand."

"And how much does the taxi to the chicken wholesaler cost?"

"Seven rand each way," answered Nozandile, who had been researching the question.

"So that means in order to buy ten chickens Nozandile needs 414 rand."

They murmured their agreement.

"Now how much will Nozandile sell her chickens for?" I wanted to know.

"Sixty rand each," said someone.

"So how much will she have when she sells all ten chickens?"

"Six hundred rand."

"So how much profit will she have to spend for herself?"

"Six hundred rand," answered a few people immediately, with big smiles on their faces at the thought of that much money.

"No! Not at all!" I said. "If she spends six hundred rand on food and new clothing for her children, how will she buy more chickens?"

There was silence. I could see my point sinking in and returned to where I had started. "How much does she need to buy ten chickens?"

"Four hundred rand."

"And for the taxi?"

"Fourteen rand."

"And how much does she need to repay me?" We hadn't agreed on a repayment plan yet so I answered my own question. "Let's say it's twenty rand each week. So how much does that leave for her?" They did the math and realized it was less than 175 rand, not bad but not a lot for a week's worth of work either. Still, I could see the lesson was working.

The big day to distribute the money came in early August. I showed up with seven thousand rand stuffed in my pocket, carefully counted out into bundles of six hundred, seven hundred, fifteen hundred, or whatever amount the loan was for. One by one, we called the women into our meeting room, reviewed the repayment schedules, the business ideas, the expenses, and handed over the money. It was difficult not to be swept up in the moment and not to have a sense that this was the beginning of something important. Their poverty wouldn't end overnight, if it ended at all, and there was still a long and difficult road ahead. But it was a moment to remember. All the meetings and classes and research made me hopeful that we were setting in motion something new, something exciting, and something that would work.

Twelve

Clothes (Un)Make the Woman

THE BORROWERS HAD A month-long grace period before their first repayments were due. I was out of town for part of this time. When I returned, there was good news. Everyone had made their first repayments and some even paid more than the agreed-upon amount. But not everything was quite as I had envisioned it.

Xoliswa had been a terrific candidate for a loan. She had once run a spaza shop out of her shack, but several years earlier her HIV had turned to AIDS and she teetered on the edge of death. She started taking antiretrovirals and returned to health, but her shop had suffered while she was sick and she no longer had the capital necessary to reopen it. Instead, she lined up every day to collect the cornmeal and bread we distributed and often visited the clinic, complaining of a headache or sore throat. Our loan to her had been fifteen hundred rand to restart the spaza shop. She had already proven she could run a shop, and the loan would help her recover what AIDS had taken away. It was an easy decision.

But there was one comment she made as we lent her the money that had given me slight pause. She took the money, counted it, smiled at me, and said something quickly in Xhosa. I asked Unathi to translate. "She says she has made *umqombothi*, Xhosa beer, to celebrate opening the new shop."

"Why?" I wanted to know.

"She hopes it will attract more people to the shop," said Unathi. I didn't want to interfere in a celebration I might not have understood, nor did I want to question her business strategy. But she hadn't mentioned selling alcohol in our planning meetings, and it wasn't hard to imagine that it could come to dominate her business. Still, she had presented us a detailed shopping list for how she would spend the fifteen hundred rand and I trusted she would do just that.

She had been one of the borrowers who was paying more than we had agreed on, and I was eager to see her shop. Climbing the hill behind the clinic one morning, I found what I feared. In a side room of her shack there were a half dozen mostly drunk men drinking Juba and *umqombothi*. They greeted me as most drunks did in Itipini by asking me for more money. I poked my head into another room and saw Xoliswa preparing another round. On one side wall were two vats of *umqombothi*. Next to them was a crate of Juba. The goods she had so carefully itemized for us were nowhere to be seen. She was running a full-blown *shebeen*, one more in a community that already had too many. Not only had she not followed through on what we had agreed, she was furthering an alcohol dependency that already generated too many health concerns and too much traffic in the clinic. By the standards of her repayments, she was one of the microcredit program's successes. But this was not at all what I had had in mind.

I smiled and asked a few questions about the business, noting casually that I didn't see any of the goods she had shown us on the list. She readily agreed and was completely unapologetic. Alcohol was what sold, and it sold well. Like any good entrepreneur she was simply providing what the market demanded—and demanded insatiably. She was profiting handsomely from it. I didn't see how my moral judgment had any impact on the goal of the microcredit program, which was to improve her standard of living. I sighed and returned to the clinic, unsure how to proceed.

Over the next few weeks and months, Xoliswa essentially vanished from the Community Project area. She no longer came regularly to the clinic complaining of minor ailments. She came once a month for the multivitamins and nutritional supplements we gave to all HIV patients. I only rarely saw her waiting in line for food. And I noticed that she more frequently had her hair done with the long braid extensions that so many women liked. Hairdressing was big business in Mthatha, I knew, and it wasn't cheap. Her life was changing as a result of the loan. Did it matter that she was using the loan to run a *shebeen*?

The other initial success story was Nobathembu, an older woman who had also opened a spaza shop, though in a different part of Itipini than Xoliswa's. Like Xoliswa, she had once been quite sick with AIDS, but in the months before the launch of the microcredit program, she had begun to take antiretrovirals and her CD4 count, which had previously been astonishingly low, began to climb and she regained her strength. I thought of her, more than any other, when I worried about the impact of a borrower's health on her business prospects. My concerns were slightly allayed by her business support partner, her son Jackson. Unlike most young men in Itipini, I knew him to be shrewd and capable of keeping an eye on the business.

In the beginning, Nobathembu was faithful in her repayments. Her spaza shop was in the heart of what I called "downtown Itipini," the oldest part of the community, where the shacks were pressed tightly against each other and the roofs were so low that I was in danger of knocking my head against the protruding pieces of tin. Because it was close to the river, mud was tracked everywhere, inside the shacks and out. Compared to the area up the hill where Xoliswa had her shop, downtown was always dirtier, smellier, and seemed more desperate. Nobathembu's spaza shop was a neat little oasis in the midst of this. Against one wall of her shack were shelves full of the goods she had for sale—little packets of sugar, paraffin for cooking, candles, some vegetables, little bags of chips, and more.

Coming to check on her progress one day, I was surprised to find her lying in bed in the middle of the morning.

"I'm cold," she groaned when she saw me. It was an answer I recognized from when Pakama had been sick and bespoke a larger weakness and lack of energy. But Nobathembu already was taking ARVs. It wasn't a good sign that her condition was deteriorating. She assured me that she was continuing to do good business and that Jackson had been helping her restock the shop. I suppressed my nervousness at the thought of how much she still had to repay—after all, she had a good location, things were selling well, and she'd already made the first repayments—and told her I'd be back to check on her soon.

Nobathembu's health only worsened, and the repayments began to come exclusively from Jackson, who had taken over the spaza shop and was also selling goods from his own home elsewhere in Itipini. I took Nobathembu to the Ngangalizwe health center to make sure she had the right ARV regimen. She did—but her health wasn't improving.

Jackson came to see Unathi and me one day, concerned. "She's using all the paraffin," he complained. "Now there isn't enough money to buy more."

Jackson had enough money that day to restock the store but I knew it wasn't a long-term solution. I went to visit Nobathembu and asked her about the paraffin. "I'm cold," she told me again. With several liters of paraffin directly in front of her, waiting to be sold, and the winter weather easily penetrating the thin walls of her shack, it wasn't hard to see that she had given in to the temptation to use the paraffin herself. I wasn't sure I would have made a different decision in the same circumstances. But it was also exactly what I had hoped to guard against with my business lessons before we lent the money. If she used the paraffin herself, she would have no money left to buy more, generate more profit, and continue to repay us. We would be dependent on Jackson's efforts and he wasn't even the official borrower.

I was puzzled about the cause of Nobathembu's poor health until I passed her one day while driving out of Itipini. She had mustered the energy to make it into town and was on her way back. When she saw me approaching in the car, she snuck her hand behind her back, attempting to hide what she was holding. But it's hard to hide a bottle of wine, especially when it comes in half gallons. The bottle was already half gone and she hadn't even made it home. If this was where her profits were going, it was no wonder her health wasn't improving. Xoliswa had opened a *shebeen*; Nobathembu was patronizing them.

Nobathembu's health continued to worsen and became a greater concern than the repayment of the loan. One of the staff was designated to bring her lunch every day when the preschool students ate. Dorothy lectured her about drinking. We made sure she was taking nutritional supplements. Something worked because, gradually, she regained her strength and stopped complaining about the cold, and her condition became less critical.

At the same time, however, Jackson clearly made the decision to divest himself of his mother's business interests. He became harder and harder to find and his repayments on her behalf tailed off. By the time Nobathembu was back to strength, whatever principal she had had from the initial loan had disappeared. I was reluctant to give her more money for another try when the first attempt had so utterly collapsed. Quietly, Unathi and I decided to let the loan die. Nobathembu was back to her old life and lined up for food each morning.

The three cell phone airtime sellers were having problems as well. The idea was fairly straightforward. They bought the airtime, wandered the streets of Mthatha in yellow vests that identified them as airtime sellers, and made a small profit on each sale. They needed a high sales volume to make enough profit each day to make it worth their while. To generate that volume, they had to be out on the streets on their feet all day, every day. I knew it would be arduous, and we talked about it with each person before we lent the money. One woman, in fact, was denied a loan because she seemed insufficiently committed to the idea. But the others made much of their enthusiasm to earn money.

That enthusiasm quickly waned, however. I saw our airtime sellers hanging around Itipini and asked them why they weren't in town. "Too hot," I heard. Or "I'm selling from home today." Evidently, they hoped people would know they sold airtime and come purchase it from their shack directly. That might generate some business but not nearly enough to make their repayments. Still, they were making their repayments so I didn't ask too many questions. The money was coming from somewhere.

But after several weeks of seeing too many airtime sellers too frequently in Itipini and not in town, I began to investigate how they were making the money. They weren't. Their repayments were coming out of the grants they received for their children. They had essentially used the microcredit program as a low-interest cash advance. We were getting repayments and could relend the money but there was no new money being generated for the borrowers, the whole purpose of the program.

I was familiar, of course, with political debates at home about whether welfare programs created a cycle of dependency. In the past, I had always thought this idea to be overblown. Why would anyone let themselves be dependent on a welfare payment? But I realized that with the airtime sellers I was seeing dependency right in front of my eyes. In most microcredit programs, the incentive to make the business a success is the constant pressure of repayment. But the grants took away that incentive. When there were too many pressing tasks at home—or it was "too hot"—they simply stopped selling airtime, confident they could make the repayment out of their grant. Their business floundered as a result. It was some small consolation to learn later that even in well-established microcredit programs, a large number of grants end up being used as cash advances and that South Africa—which, with its social welfare system, is unusual in the developing world—has never had many successful microcredit programs. But it was still a disappointment.

I had the greatest hope for Nozandile, the chicken seller who had been the example in the class on business principles. It was, to my mind, the most creative of the ideas, and Nozandile had shown a firm understanding of what it would take to be a success. She had convinced me that there was a big market for chickens in Itipini and that the potential profits were great. The first time I went to see her, there were half a dozen live chickens exploring the nooks and crannies of her shack. She had a big smile on her face when I asked how business was going.

"I've sold four already and other people have expressed interest in these ones," she said, indicating the chickens at her feet. She had only purchased the chickens that morning so they were selling quickly.

It was good news and I asked when she would go again.

"Next month, when people pay me," she responded.

"Next month, Nozandile!" I exclaimed. "The chickens are going to sell faster than that. The more often you go, the more money you will make."

"But people won't pay me until they get paid at the end of the month or on the fifteenth."

My knowledge of local business practices wasn't sufficient to understand what she was saying. "What do you mean?" I asked.

"People get their grants and their paychecks at the end of the month or on the fifteenth. They took the chickens now but they will only give me the money when they get paid."

I hadn't considered the possibility of selling on credit. I had blithely assumed that before Nozandile handed over a chicken, the person would give her the cash. "Nozandile, what if they do not pay you?"

"I only sell to people I trust. If they do not pay, I will not sell again." That was hopeful. If they didn't repay her, the strategy could bankrupt her and prevent her from having the opportunity to sell more chickens.

Moreover, if customers were paying at different times in the month, she would have to hang on to a substantial amount of cash for a few weeks. I knew she knew the importance of setting aside the capital to be able to continue to buy more chickens. But I worried what would happen on a hungry night when there was a ready pile of cash around. Her profit margin on each trip was not huge, and she needed to make trips to the chicken farm more frequently than once a month to start generating the kind of income we both hoped for. But I held back. She knew better than I did how business worked in Itipini, and buying and selling on credit seemed to be fairly common practice. She made her first few repayments and I didn't see any reason to harass her further.

In designing the program, I had had some romantic idea that my work stopped once Unathi and I lent the money. Hardly. Checking on the microcredit borrowers became another task to add to my list. When friends and family back home heard about the program, they were eager to send money to expand it. But I didn't need more money. I needed people—people who could check on borrowers, coach them through setting up a business, and motivate them to get to work. Unathi and I were strained with just the dozen or so we had. Financial resources were fine. But social and human resources were more impor-tant—and most lacking.

The system wasn't perfect but there was some discernible prog-ress—even if it wasn't always as I had imagined—in the lives of the bor-rowers. If people were making their repayments—and most still were—I couldn't see much to complain about. The trouble was when Yoliswa stopped.

✍

Two weeks after her first repayment, Yoliswa showed up in Itipini and asked to speak with me privately. I knew immediately it was bad news. If the business was going well, she would have no trouble talking about it with me in public.

We went into a side room and sat down. "I am in trouble," she said, wearily. My heart sank.

"What's wrong?" I asked, trying to be upbeat.

"My aunt says she doesn't want to support me anymore. She doesn't make enough money to feed all of us and she doesn't want me around. I can't live there anymore."

"What will you do?" I asked, thinking not for the first or last time how I wished the magnitude of the problems people felt comfortable discussing with me would grow at the same pace as my ability to handle them.

"I don't know. I don't know where to live." Her head was bowed and she was weeping.

"You could move back to Itipini with your mother," I suggested. Even as I said it, I knew it would destroy her business. It would move her too far away from her market in Chris Hani.

"I. Am. Not. Coming back here," she said, clenching her teeth through her tears. I was taken aback by the vehemence with which she said it.

"Could you offer to help pay your aunt some money to stay with her?"

"I don't have any money," she said, continuing to cry.

"Yes, you do. You've been making money selling clothes. If you took some of your profit and gave it to your aunt maybe you could continue to live with her." I started writing down some numbers on a piece of paper, figuring out how it could work.

The idea wasn't gaining much traction, I could tell, and Yoliswa still looked worried. I didn't know if it was a sign that the business wasn't going well.

"All right," I asked, wanting to try another tack. "How much would it cost to live on your own?"

She started listing the figures and it immediately became clear that there was no way she could make that happen. I gently suggested Itipini again. Again, she firmly resisted.

I left the conversation there. I had made some suggestions but they weren't taking root. There were other people who needed my attention that day. More than that, however, I couldn't let myself admit that Yoliswa might be failing. I had written about her in letters back home. I wasn't mentally prepared for the fact that my star borrower might be about to turn to failure. And the truth was, I didn't know what story I would tell to replace hers.

That conversation was the last I saw of Yoliswa before I left Mthatha for a few weeks. I had said I would try to visit her one last time to say goodbye but I didn't. I told myself I didn't have time, but the reality was that I didn't want to confront failure. I was making progress in Itipini, finally moving from *being* to actually *doing* something. I needed to think she was doing well so I could have some sort of success to keep me going. We had previously made arrangements for Yoliswa to make repayments to a friend of mine in my absence. One way of looking at it is that I had done what I could and needed to let others do the work. Another way of looking at it is I ran away, fearful of acknowledging the reality of the situation.

When I returned, my friend told me that Yoliswa hadn't made any repayments. I was prepared for the news but it still wasn't what I wanted to hear. I had lots of people to look in on in Itipini. Visiting Yoliswa kept getting pushed further and further down my priority list. It was pushed so far down it never happened. I couldn't bring myself to visit Yoliswa's house. She didn't call me. The repayments were never made.

Driving by Chris Hani one Sunday afternoon, I heard someone shout my name. I knew immediately who it was, but it still took me a moment to look in the mirror and confirm it. Yoliswa was standing on the side of the road, waving after me. It took another moment for me to decide to turn around—I could pretend I never heard her, I told myself—and circle back. It had been so long since I had seen her that I hardly knew where to begin.

"How are you, Yoliswa?" I asked.

"I'm fine," she said in a voice that suggested otherwise.

"How are your children?" I said, dodging the opportunity to learn more about her.

"Sisipho and Sikhokele are living in Itipini with my mother. Bongamusa is here."

"Where are you living?"

"Over there," she said, pointing away from where her aunt's house had been.

We carried on our desultory and torturous small talk for a few more moments. I couldn't bring myself to ask where the money was—it was gone, I knew—or how the clothes selling was going or with whom she was living. Eventually, I cut it short: "Well, I need to go do some work now."

"Okay, see you around."

We both knew I was blowing her off. As I drove away, I knew why: I couldn't deal with the failure.

A few months passed and I tried not to think about Yoliswa. I assumed she had taken the principal of the loan and used it to find a new place to live. I could easily see how in such a difficult time the idea of selling clothes—and making money in the future—had slipped away as she confronted her current, pressing needs. I didn't blame her for the decision. But I still wished she hadn't made it.

In December, not long before Christmas, I was driving through town and saw Yoliswa walking out of the police station. She saw me and called my name.

The traffic was slowing down so I rolled down my window and shouted back, "How are you?"

"Yho!" she said, using an all-purpose South African expression. "Not good! My boyfriend has beaten me up."

The boyfriend must have been new, and it explained whom she had been living with after her aunt asked her to leave. It made me think of her marriage proposal so many months earlier and how she summarized the Disney books for me. I was distraught that someone I once cared for was in such a situation. There was so much I wanted to tell her and so much I wanted to hear from her. I might have slowed down. I might have gotten out of the car. But our past failure too deeply colored the relationship. The traffic was speeding up again. I waved a goodbye out the window and tried to forget I had seen her.

I took Yoliswa's failure to get her business off the ground as a personal failure. If I had somehow worked harder, helped her prepare differently, or intervened earlier or more often, I told myself, the results would have been different. I knew that there were outside factors at work but didn't let myself dwell on them. Solipsistically, I dwelt on my own failure. It was a searing experience.

How many other people in South Africa and around the developing world have the same problem? Surely there are people who are committed to improving living conditions. They start with a good idea, lay the groundwork, and plan for it. They do research and make sure that everyone is on board with the idea. They launch their intervention, ready for it to take wing and improve living conditions. Instead, they watch helplessly as it crashes back to earth. The transition from overwhelming hope to complete despair is sudden and crushing. After a few failures, might they—me—not start to think that it was time to give up even trying? Why bother to do anything if it is just going to fail in the end? No matter how hard we tried to keep the sun shining in the sky, it seemed, we were powerless to stop the night from coming.

I didn't want to let the failure affect me. But it was. I tried to invest myself in other projects and concentrate on developing new success stories. Some of the other borrowers weren't doing that poorly. A few of the students were showing marked improvement in their English. There was Pakama and a growing list of people like her. But I couldn't get away from Yoliswa. I had been in South Africa a year and a half. It was getting to be time to think about leaving.

Thirteen

"On This Rock . . ."

THE CHOIR MKUSELI CONDUCTED after school was nominally made up of students but I called it "the young mother's club." They were all of student age—and a few were actually still in school—but most had dropped out of school when they gave birth. Rehearsals were an odd sight. Mkuseli directed his singers while their children crawled around and between them. They practiced in the same shipping container we used for English class, and performed at community events like the pre-school graduation. Before I arrived, the choir had recorded a CD that sold well among donors to African Medical Mission and given choir members a chance at fame in Itipini. In October of my second year, it was time to record a second CD. We set off for Grahamstown, a university town about five hours away with a recording studio we had booked.

There had been some turnover in the choir since the previous CD, so as it happened I was driving many people in the van as far from Mthatha as they had ever been. Grahamstown is clean and posh and the students oohed and ahhed as we drove down its main street, gazing in wonder at the freshly manicured lawns of Rhodes University, one of South Africa's finest. On the drive home, we stopped at the ocean and went for a swim. For many in the group, it was the first time they had seen the ocean, even though it is a mere hour away from Mthatha and a place I visited on occasional weekends.

There were only three men on the trip—myself, Mkuseli, and Petros, a young man of about twenty who held down the tenor line solo—which meant one of us got to spend the overnight in his own room at the bed and breakfast. I offered it to Mkuseli. With a sprawling queen-size bed, hardwood floors, and French doors that opened onto a patio, it was larger than his home in Mthatha. When I went to see how he was doing, I wasn't sure I'd be able to get him to leave the next morning.

I roomed with Petros and he was terrific. He was helpful and thoughtful during the entire trip and went to bed early. In the morning, he neatly made his bed and arranged his pillow. I left mine in a jumble of sheets for the maid. None of this was unsurprising. Petros was a gentle and genuinely helpful person. His demeanor—and his carefully tended dreadlocks—had made him stand out from the mass of people I met when I first arrived. Like so many other young men, he was unemployed then and not in school. Robert, a previous volunteer, had taken a liking to Petros and involved him in the life of the Community Project. Watching him work—finding records in the clinic, dispensing medicines, and sorting out the line of patients—it was clear that he had an innate intelligence. His record wasn't spotless, however. In his late teens, Petros spent several months in jail because he had been caught by police in a stolen car. Because of the language barrier and the general embarrassment about talking about such events, I never got the exact details of the story.

After Robert left, the expectation seemed to be that I should carry on the relationship with Petros. There was a strong case for doing so. When patients' names stymied my best efforts to find their records, I asked for his help. When I tried to communicate with a patient and couldn't, Petros's English was good enough to interpret. He often accompanied me on my trips to the hospital or into town and was a great help. He willingly lifted sick patients in and out of the truck and helped them find their way around the warren of hallways in the hospital.

But there was another part of Petros I had more trouble with. On our drives back to Itipini, he'd turn the radio up and sit, sullenly listening to driving, pulsing African dance music. I didn't know what to say so we sat in silence, listening to the throbbing beats and stewing in our collective discomfort. Petros didn't have a job, I knew, but I had come to Africa to save people. Beyond finding him a job, which was out of my reach anyway, it didn't seem like Petros needed much saving. If that was the case, I thought, what good was he? The thought that, perhaps, he could be helpful in saving others never seemed to register. I didn't know what Petros wanted or how I could provide it.

In those early days in Itipini, I was well used to frustration—at the language barrier, at feeling ineffective or useless—so to be frustrated in my relationship with Petros was nothing new. What was new, however, was how I began to channel my frustration toward and at Petros. He didn't deserve it. We weren't meshing in the way he had with Robert but that didn't seem like reason enough to dread his very presence. His detachment in the car wasn't unlike that of the other young men in the community, unsure how to act around the new, tall, white man. I found myself beginning to hope he wouldn't show up in the morning. I deluded myself into thinking that I could do anything he could, which was definitively not true, and could do it better—also not true. Petros got my unspoken message. His appearances in the clinic became more and more sporadic.

Petros's name always reminded me of the passage in the Gospel of Matthew when Peter names Jesus as the Messiah. Jesus replies, "And I tell you, you are Peter, and on this rock I will build my church." When I took Greek, I learned that Jesus is making a pun on Peter's Greek name, Petros, which is also the Greek word for rock. I have always interpreted the passage as indicating Jesus' preference for the outcast and lowly of society, like the fishermen and tax collectors that Peter and his fellow apostles were. If Jesus had a preference for these kinds of people—and could build a church out of them—surely I should as well, right? When I gave Petros the cold shoulder, his very name reminded me of the unbiblical nature of my action. Perhaps he was just the kind of rock that Jesus preferred.

Eventually, Petros's appearances dropped off entirely and he was nowhere to be found. The story that went around said he had severely beaten up another young man and had fled the community for his safety for a while. Like so much else that happened in Itipini, I never learned all the details. It was hard to know what to make of him. Clearly, he had talent and skill. Why would he do something like this? But he was gone, and the pressure of the daily crisis in the clinic had a way of taking my focus off of him. His absence wasn't the worst thing in the world.

By the time Petros wandered back into the Community Project many weeks later, the room that the students in the after-school program used as their gym—a few sets of weights, a ping-pong table, and a punching bag—had acquired a new item: a billiards table. The room was primarily meant for students but several young men prevailed on Mkuseli to open the room in the morning and let them play. It quickly turned into a hangout spot for a small crowd of young men, shooting pool and lifting weights.

It was possible to see this as a fairly good thing. The room was drug-free so there was at least a part of their day when these young men weren't smoking and drinking. Their fun did seem to be genuine. But I couldn't help developing a growing distaste for them. I knew there were few formal jobs to be had, but many older men in Itipini set off into town each day to make some money, or try to at least. Moreover, I knew that several of the young men were fathers to children in the preschool and that some had girlfriends who were HIV positive. But I was a better father to the preschool children, it seemed, than these pool-playing layabouts, none of whom had ever been tested for HIV. I thought I had learned enough in life and in Itipini not to succumb to the temptation to blame the poor for their own circumstances. But distaste came easily to someone who was white, educated, and had never been hungry. I had passed on more opportunities than these men had ever been offered.

Objectively, I knew all this. But with each passing encounter it became easier and easier to find reasons not to like these young men and invent new reasons why the situation was their own fault. I thought the little knowledge I had gained gave me the opportunity to judge the rights and wrongs of life in a community I had only been a part of for a little while. My scorn was a sign of my confidence in Itipini. I wandered out of the clinic and stared in at their pool game, knowing that my presence made them uncomfortable, but feeling smugly self-satisfied nonetheless.

Petros joined the pool-playing crowd when he returned to Itipini, and on one of my visits he approached me as soon as I walked in. "Jesse, we are hungry. Give us money for food." This was not an uncommon request from young men either in town or in Itipini. My response to Petros was even less charitable than it was to the young men who asked me for money while standing in front of the *shebeens*.

"You're hungry? Then why are you playing pool? I'm not going to give you money for food when you're playing pool all morning."

Petros had a ready answer for that: "Okay, let's make a plan for food." "Making a plan" was an expression he had picked up from Jenny in the clinic, who used it when sorting through complicated situations.

"Alright," I said, my voice rising in self-righteous indignation. "My plan would begin with putting down the pool cues and going into town to find work." I knew it was naive but it felt good to say. Petros and his friends snorted. It was clear there was no work to be had. My comment ended the conversation. I stalked out and returned to the clinic, feeling satisfied and sanctimonious. At least there was one young man in Itipini who was working!

☙

In my less smug moments, when the young men weren't directly in front of me, I allowed that it wasn't healthy or helpful just to get frustrated at Petros and the pool players. Lots of people in Itipini aggravated me but I was usually able to overcome that initial feeling. Yet I struggled with the young men. When I talked about Itipini and showed pictures while raising money at home, people would ask, "Where are all the men?" My pictures were dominated by women and children. The men weren't around often enough to wander into my camera frame. I responded that it was my goal for my second year in Itipini to get to know more men better. It made me sound reasonable and mature, I thought, but deep inside I knew I had no idea how I would begin. I wasn't even sure I really wanted to. After all, I had tried with Petros—more or less—and not made it very far.

Rather than reducing the requests for money, the launch of the microcredit program set a lot of people thinking about new ways to get money from me. A group of young men banded together to write a business plan. They wanted to make and sell soap and candles. I should have been overjoyed: here was a ready-made way to come to know a group of young men, and it fit neatly into the microcredit framework. Instead, I approached the project with the usual mixture of trepidation and smugness.

The group had written a "constitution," in English, the first article of which was that all decisions should be made by the whole group. There were sixteen names on their membership roster. I sent word around that we would have an initial meeting on a Tuesday. My messenger to the group looked eager and said they hoped for the money by Friday. I assured him it would not happen that quickly and that it would definitely not happen at all if the first meeting never took place.

Unathi was away but my friend Noxolo came to the meeting to hear about the plan. Four young men showed up. I pointed to the first article of the constitution and said we couldn't make any decisions. Since I had them there, however, I asked them to explain their idea and how it would work. One young man I had never met before stepped forward and articulately explained what they wanted to do. "We want to help ourselves, to create some work because there is no work. We want to make some goods and sell them and make money." It was a good line, no doubt the one he thought I wanted to hear.

I was well into the microcredit frame of mind at this point so I pressed him on the idea. "How much will it cost for the wax to make candles?"

There was silence. No one knew. I feigned tiredness, like they were wasting my time, and told them the first step was to go into town and find out.

"Who will you sell to?" I asked next.

They had a one-word answer: "Jenny." Some of the older women who worked at the Project made beaded keychains and necklaces in the afternoon when the workday ended. Occasionally, they sold them to visitors or Jenny or me when we needed gifts. But it functioned primarily as a social circle and not as an income-generating enterprise.

"Really!" I exclaimed sarcastically. "How many candles do you think Jenny needs? How much money can you make with that?"

"We'll sell to people in the community as well," one young man added quickly.

"Will they buy candles? How many candles do they use a week? Can you make candles for cheaper than they sell in town?" I fired off my questions in quick succession. I was being overly aggressive but they were exactly the same questions I had asked—more gently—of the other microcredit borrowers.

The young men didn't have many good answers. It wasn't clear there were many to be had. Like many other basic consumer goods, candles are very cheap in Mthatha. It was hard to see the wisdom of starting a business in Itipini that couldn't undersell cheap Chinese imports. But they promised to do some research and add more figures to their business plan.

A week went by and I didn't hear a word from them. Finally, I asked around about what had happened. I found one young man, who hadn't been at the first meeting and who seemed a little unsure what was going on, even though his name was on the initial list. We repeated our conversation from the first meeting and he promised to talk to the others and do the research.

It was the last I heard of the idea. A few weeks later when I thought of it again and asked around, Noxolo told me, "They wanted you to give them the money at the first meeting and you didn't." It wasn't said in an accusatory way and I knew she wasn't blaming me for the failure of the group. The young men had seen how I was funding other projects and wanted some of that money for themselves. I wanted to help but also wanted them to prove their seriousness. Evidently, my first and most basic tests had proven insurmountable.

The position Petros and these young men found themselves in—no work, no money, little education, and few options for the future—is not unique. The role of men in Xhosa society has been changing dramatically in the last few generations, and they are caught in the middle of it. At one time, the ideal Xhosa male was a rural patriarch of a large family with a *kraal* of several huts, a herd of cows, and children to inherit his name and possessions. A man's cows were his wealth and were used to pay the *lobola* or bride-price so that he could be formally married. In his autobiography, Nelson Mandela describes growing up in the rural Transkei and learning at the feet of these male leaders in the community. But that lifestyle is evaporating. Before and during apartheid, the need for male labor in the mines near Johannesburg drained the region of its men. In the democratic era, the process has only continued, though now rural men are moving to urban centers like Mthatha in search of work and opportunities they cannot find in a rural village. A Xhosa boy growing up today would have a much different story to tell than Mandela's.

As the ideal of being a rural patriarch has dissolved, another has risen to take its place. A common culture, disseminated through television, radios, newspapers, and billboards, shows men being providers for their families. They are manly men and tough. American wrestling shows and soap operas—and the gender roles they perpetuate—are popular all over the country. A major beer company's billboard shows a brawny man working hard in a steel mill under the slogan, "You deserve a Carling." Many men might think they deserve a beer but few of them have jobs to afford it or support their families.

At the same time that this new masculinity has grown in prominence, it has become harder and harder to achieve. Old methods of generating wealth—like farming or rearing cattle—no longer work, but there are few jobs to generate income. The education needed to get those jobs is more expensive and more limited. Even when people do get education, they often can't find jobs with their new qualifications. I knew university graduates who had difficulty finding work.

The result is not simply that there are a number of unemployed young men hanging around during the day. They are also looking for ways to assert their masculinity. One alternative is crime. South Africa's astronomical crime statistics are due to many things, but one thing they make clear is that far too many young men are choosing this option. I was once approached by a young woman who pleaded with me to help her boyfriend find work. Otherwise, she feared, he would become a *tsotsi*. If *tsotsis* are the model that boys are aspiring to, then going to school hardly helps them in their goals.

Aside from crime, about the only other way young men in Itipini can assert their masculinity is through sex. One of the young men in Itipini who played pool was the recent father of twins. When they were born, he strutted around with pride and accepted the congratulations of his friends. But he didn't seem much invested in the care of his children, and when one of the twins died six weeks after birth, he was nowhere to be found. Sex with multiple partners allowed men to assert their manhood in the face of societal circumstances that only serve to emasculate them. Yet in an era of an HIV epidemic spread almost entirely by heterosexual intercourse, the result is mass tragedy. There wasn't a huge distance between the young men in the poolroom and the gaunt, weak, and dying ones I helped navigate the antiretroviral system. The one source of power remaining to men results in the sickness and death that is decimating their generation.

The old ways of thinking no longer apply and the ideas of manhood and masculinity need to be rethought so there can be a new and healthy way to be a productive man in Xhosa culture. I was raised initially by a stay-at-home father and taught at a young age that men and women were equally capable and responsible, so I had my own thoughts on the matter. But I also knew enough to know that it wasn't for an outsider like me to be doing the rethinking. That impetus had to come from within the culture itself. In Itipini, I saw no signs that it was happening.

☙

There was a bittersweet sense, then, as I watched Petros make his bed on the choir trip. He was innately talented and capable. But I had also seen how he didn't always respond to the challenges around him in the most helpful way. As we drove back to Mthatha in the quiet, tired glow of a successful trip, I mentally kicked myself for being so exclusionary in the past and resolved to work with him anew.

Two weeks after we returned, before I even had a chance to try again with Petros, there was tragic news. Petros and a friend had been arrested for the murder of another young man. My reaction to the news came simultaneously on many levels. The immediate one was shock and revulsion. But there was also profound disappointment that these two young men should end up in a situation when there was so much potential for a different future. Most of all, it was deeply unsettling how well I knew Petros. The murder had happened a few weeks earlier, and when I did the math I realized that Petros and I had roomed together after the crime. I was careful to withhold judgment on his guilt, but it was also discomfiting to have shared a room with someone implicated in such a way.

My daily commute took me past Wellington jail on the outskirts of Mthatha but I only ever paid it occasional interest, usually when it made the news. There were not infrequent prison breaks and a local newspaper called it one of the worst in the country. The newspaper said it was "a prison hellhole," overflowing with prisoners, where HIV spread rapidly and those awaiting trial and those already convicted mingled freely. Now as I drove past the prison, I thought of Petros inside. The wheels of justice in Mthatha, such as they were, creaked along slowly. His sister told me that in his first week in prison, Petros had been brought into town for several preliminary hearings but they had all been postponed because the docket was overwhelmed. Petros very likely faced the possibility of spending a great deal of time in prison prior to any trial.

Each day I drove past, I thought about turning into Wellington to see if I could be let in to visit Petros. I hadn't exactly followed Biblical mandates in my past relationship with Petros, but regardless of his guilt or innocence, there seemed to be a pretty clear case for paying him a visit. But the concerns built in my mind. I was worried Petros or his family might expect me to give him things on each visit. I didn't want to be reduced—again—to the role of the white person who only handed out stuff. That was not what interested me anymore, if it ever had. Visiting Petros also meant venturing into a new part of town, one that had a fairly fearsome reputation as far as I was concerned. Beyond that, there were numerous logistical challenges to consider—when were the visiting hours? What kind of ID did I need? Did I have to be on some kind of preapproved list to visit Petros? I did some sporadic reconnaissance. A retired nun I knew had visited Wellington frequently during her ministry. She told me I didn't have to worry about any of the logistics. In her visits, she had found it "quite well run." That was all I needed to know. If she could do it, so could I.

I took a morning off from the clinic one Wednesday to arrive at the beginning of the visiting hours. As I drove through the gates, my heart beating in anticipation and nervousness, I was impressed by the prison grounds. A few towering trees shaded the road, and the grounds were clean and manicured. It was quite the contrast to the chaotic and dirty streets of Mthatha. The prison looked like I might have imagined: big lights, tall watchtowers, heavy gates, plenty of barbed wire. It left me wondering how so many prisoners escaped. Then I met the guards. They seemed to be manning their posts rather casually, not notably focused on the job at hand. It was the same lackadaisical approach to work I was familiar with in Mthatha, but in a prison it made for an unnerving sight.

My reconnaissance had failed to learn just where in the prison Petros was being held. I headed for the maximum-security part of the prison complex, reasoning it was an appropriate place to put someone charged with murder. But as a prisoner awaiting trial, Petros was being held in the medium-security prison. By the time I learned all this from bored and distracted prison guards who couldn't seem to tell me who was being held where, the time I had allotted myself had run out and I was needed back in Itipini.

Buoyed by the experience of having breached the prison walls, so to speak, I returned not long afterwards with Petros' sister in tow. We made it into the medium security prison, through the gates and past the guards, and into the visiting room. One long glass wall separated visitors from detainees and small groups clustered on one side to speak to their prisoner through a small cluster of holes. Petros was waiting at the end of the room, a hopeful and expectant look on his face. He looked healthy and well fed.

It was hard to know what to say and even harder to hear or make myself understood. Our words vanished into the air around us, and the other nearby conversations were distracting. As a result, I didn't say much at all. I asked how he was being treated and told him a few things that had happened in Itipini. He talked about how he watched a lot of television and had a little time outside each day. Otherwise, he seemed quite bored. Mostly, I just let Petros and his sister catch up in Xhosa. We had just begun reading *The BFG* in the after-school English class, and I had a few copies left over. I knew Petros would be able to read it and I asked if he'd like a copy. When I mentioned the idea, his eyes brightened. It was a reason for me to come back and it was a gift I could feel good about giving.

I returned a week later with not only *The BFG* but also some spare copies of other books that had been floating around the library. I had been thinking about what I would want to do if I was in prison. For me, the obvious answer was to write. So, in the worst kind of projection, I brought along some writing paper and pens for Petros. On the first page, I wrote him a note telling him I knew he was smart and could read and write. If he wanted to, I suggested, he should use some of his time to write down what he was thinking. In a brief flight of fancy, I dreamed of Petros writing of his experiences in a *Narrative of the Life of Frederick Douglass* kind of way. Maybe, I reasoned, at this moment of his greatest need, he would begin to turn his life around. Maybe, having failed so utterly to relate to him, I could now play an instrumental role and save him from this prison and these circumstances. It was romantic nonsense better suited to Hollywood than Mthatha but it gave me a small amount of hope. Not so for the guard checking the gifts. She gave me a funny look when I handed her the books and paper as if to say, "What, no food or toothpaste?" and read my note to Petros with a look of bewilderment on her face. But she handed them through the window to Petros and I went to meet him at the glass wall.

He still looked well and I could tell he was buoyed by the gifts. I tried to explain the note I had written but the glass wall made it hard to communicate in more than a few sentences at a time.

I could tell he wanted more. "Jesse," he asked. "I need some soap." It was a familiar look on his face. I'd seen it in the after-school gym when he asked for money for food.

I tried to be firm in my reply. "Petros, your mother works at the Project and makes money. If you need soap, you can ask her. I can give you books but that is all."

At that moment, the guards abruptly announced they were ending the visiting hours. It was too early and I thought about protesting but I knew it would do nothing. Petros and I looked at each other with resigned looks on our faces. Neither had gotten what we wanted out of the other. Looking at him, I realized how foolish my plans had been in the first place. I wished him luck, told him to enjoy the books and to write if he could, and left.

Fourteen

Back Where I Started

THE HIGH SCHOOL ENGLISH class kept on rolling through the school year. When we finished *Charlie and the Chocolate Factory*, we turned to *Charlotte's Web*. My rapport with the students had grown, and there was a consistent group of eight or ten who came twice a week to read. Even better, it was clear that a few of them had improved their English substantially and were doing reasonably well in school. At the end of the year, more than half of the students passed. In other parts of the world, this would be no cause for celebration. But given all the responsibilities these young women had at home and the poor quality of the school they attended, I actually found the results to be encouraging. They were certainly no worse—and maybe even a little better—than the average for the high school as a whole. Even better, some of the students were enthusiastic about school, and a couple who failed were determined to try again.

As a result, by the time my second January in Mthatha rolled around and a new crop of students came looking for help with high school, I was feeling more confident and capable than I had a year earlier while dodging raindrops with five students outside the Department of Home Affairs. The new students were notably different to the prior year's. There were seven new students for grade ten. Astonishingly, three of the seven students were male and none of the young women had children. It was a collection of students that would not have seemed that out of place at the middle-class high school I graduated from.

I put my experience to work with the new students. Before we went shopping for school supplies and uniforms, I made each of them write a list of the items they needed and made a point of reviewing and approving each one before we even left Itipini and set foot in a store. It substantially cut down the number of "Oh, but I need this too!" purchases. I had a better idea of what was needed to register at the high school, and I made sure they filled out and handed in the registration forms at the same time. In the first few weeks of school, I didn't see many slinking into the clinic during the school day complaining about a headache and asking for an excuse note. There was energy and enthusiasm and I was determined to keep the momentum going. We set right in on Roald Dahl's *The BFG,* and the students quickly took to the story of a young girl and a friendly giant. I felt competent, like I knew what I was doing and people could justifiably look to me for advice and help on beginning high school. I temporarily forgot that Nozuko High School was deeply underresourced and that none of the students spoke English all that well. Instead, I stood at the beginning of the year and saw only the horizon of possibility.

The greatest potential was in Nolizwi, the student I knew least well. I didn't know her from previous encounters around Itipini but she quickly stood out from the rest. She was more articulate—in English—than the other students and was the first to have the answers to the comprehension questions I asked. But she was also quite shy. When the other students were chatting before class, she sat quietly observing conversations but not participating. When I tried to draw her into conversations, however, she came readily, answering my questions with a transparency and forthrightness I hadn't learned to expect from the other students.

Her shyness no doubt stemmed from her recent arrival in Itipini. She had completed grade nine the previous year in a rural village some distance from Mthatha. But, she told me, her mother had become quite sick, so the family decided to send Nolizwi to Itipini to live with her uncle and his family. Nolizwi didn't say as much but it was easy to guess that her mother was HIV positive. Her uncle and his family were well known to us in the clinic. Their shack was a sprawling collection of rooms built at random to house his prodigious and ever-growing family—a wife, eight daughters ranging in age from five to eighteen, and a growing collection of grandchildren. Nolizwi had moved in with them just before the school year began. Despite the change in circumstances, she was a hard worker in school and set about her assignments with a laudable determination and drive. I saw her a few days a week when we read *The BFG* but otherwise assumed that things were going well for her.

A month into the school year, I was surprised to see Nolizwi in the circle at our morning prayers. I didn't think she would intentionally skip school and she didn't look sick so I knew something must be wrong. She made a beeline for me after the last Amen. "I have to talk to you," she said. We withdrew to a side room and it was clear she was on the verge of tears. We sat down together and she paused, biting her lip and clearly trying to figure out how to say what she wanted to in English. Finally, her story came out. She would start in halting English, stall, and switch into a torrent of Xhosa. I had to keep asking her to repeat herself.

Her mother had been discharged from the hospital a week or so earlier. When her uncle's family had learned of this, they asked Nolizwi to leave since they assumed that their duty to extend hospitality to a family member in distress was fulfilled. But Nolizwi's mother was in no shape to run a household or support her children. Anyway, Nolizwi wanted to continue to go to school in Mthatha and not start all over again in her village. Looking to stay reasonably close to the high school, she had moved to Corana, a neighborhood on the edge of Mthatha, across the river from Itipini, where she was living with a distant relation, an older woman who was from the same village and knew Nolizwi's mother. She had a long walk to school—about three miles—and every day she had to cross a narrow bridge over a river. I knew the bridge and I knew it had a reputation for being unsafe. *Tsotsis* would hang out near it and relieve solo travelers of their cell phones and other belongings.

That was exactly what had happened to Nolizwi the day before. On her way home, she had been robbed at knifepoint by a young man who took her phone and all the school supplies she had. It was clear that this was the final straw for her. She was unhappy living so far from school and walking along unsafe roads. It was sapping her considerable determination to stay in school. She wiped the tears from her eyes as she finished her story and turned to me with an expectant look on her face. I saw in her eyes the unasked question: How can you help me?

I was getting used to the idea that people in Itipini would share important moments in their lives with me but her plea opened up new territory. I'd worked on microcredit and health and education issues, but I'd never helped anyone with housing before. I wanted to be able to take as a given the fact that the people I encountered had homes—albeit in shacks—to return to each day, just as I did. A few weeks earlier, I had been operating in a comfortable zone of knowledge for the first time in a long time. Now, Nolizwi had pushed me into a new zone of ignorance. Still, she was so talented and hardworking that I deeply wanted to help her. She seemed like an obvious candidate for saving. Replacing the school supplies she had lost wasn't a problem, but it was clear that it wouldn't be a permanent solution. She still needed to make that same walk twice a day. The days were shortening so each walk would be colder and darker.

As a first step, I asked Unathi, the part-time social worker, to investigate. She returned with bad news. Nolizwi's uncle and aunt wanted nothing to do with her. Because she was a student, she couldn't contribute her share of chores, like the other older sisters could, not a single one of whom was in school. As a result, Nolizwi had become one more mouth to feed in an already stretched household. The importance of education was clearly lost on a family that was struggling to make it from day to day. Unathi offered to provide Nolizwi with cornmeal and bread from our daily distribution for HIV patients, but even that didn't convince her aunt and uncle to help. Nolizwi's mother was no longer in the hospital. Nolizwi could take care of herself.

But Unathi had an idea. One of the staff had a daughter who lived in a new government housing project and had extra space in her house. After some investigation, Unathi reported that the daughter, Asiphe, would be happy to welcome Nolizwi into her home. In fact, Asiphe's cousin also lived there and was a student at Nozuko High School. They would be able to go to school together in the morning. It seemed like a good fit. We made the introductions one afternoon after school and everyone seemed to hit it off. Once my awkward Xhosa and I got out of the way, there were smiles all around and plans were made as to when Nolizwi could move her things into the new house.

It was an encouraging development but it gave me pause as I sat on the side of the room. Even though I hadn't done much to make this happen, everyone involved knew what I wanted—a new, safe place for Nolizwi to live—and knew that keeping me happy was a good thing. I had Jenny's ear about how the Community Project ran and I had the power of being white, educated, and rich. Were the smiles and warm words only a show put on for my benefit, to satisfy me that the problem had been "solved"? To what extent did anyone here feel they were freely making a decision and could deny a request of mine if they wanted to? It was a substantial commitment they were making. Would it be sustainable were I to leave, as I knew I would be in the not too distant future? But I quickly suppressed these questions. I wanted a solution to this problem and this looked like a promising one.

On her walk home from school the following day, Nolizwi was stopped by the same *tsotsi* who had robbed her at knifepoint the week earlier. This time, he tried a different tactic and asked her to be his girlfriend. She refused and began to walk away. He chased after her and demanded her cell phone. "You took it last time!" she shouted in response and ran away. We laughed as she told me the story. She wouldn't have to do that walk for much longer.

The next week, after we had finished *The BFG* for the day, I drove with Nolizwi to collect her things from the house in Corana. As we bumped along the rutted road, she pointed out to me the dangerous points of her daily walk and the places where she tried to find someone else to walk with and seek safety in numbers. Corana isn't far from town and there was a nice view of the modest Mthatha skyline, but it still felt deeply rural and agrarian. The sun was gently sliding towards the horizon as we pulled in front of the little compound of mud-brick buildings Nolizwi had been staying in. There were chickens in the yard and a pen where a few cows would spend the night when they returned from the fields. The yard was well swept and a few small children shyly looked at me. I could see for miles across the rolling hills of the Transkei and drank in the scenery, marveling at the contrast between the beauty of the place and the danger of living here. Nolizwi went to pack her things and I chatted with her distant relation, "Granny." She was in a wheelchair, cooking in the main room of the house. There was a cooking area in one corner and an empty bed against a far wall. "Jesse," Granny asked me. "This wheelchair is old. How do I get a new one?" I had had some experience procuring wheelchairs in the past and explained the part of the hospital to visit to order a new one. Still waiting for Nolizwi, I stepped outside again to admire the scenery, feeling upbeat and positive about how well everything was going. I daydreamed a bit about how Nolizwi would be an even better student than she already was when she lived closer to school.

Granny called to me again and I poked my head in an open window over the bed. As I did, I realized the bed was not, in fact, empty. There was someone lying in it. I looked down to greet him. He could barely turn his head to respond. His chest was barely moving and his eyes were already sunk deep in their sockets. The sleeves of his shirt had fallen back enough to reveal stick-thin wrists, limply placed on top of the blanket. It was a sight that was all too familiar to me. I was no diagnostician but it was clear that he had an advanced case of AIDS.

It was not exactly what I wanted to see at that particular moment in time. There was one purpose to this trip and that was to help Nolizwi move. I had found someone I could save and she was my focus. It was nice to be able to dispense some advice about wheelchairs along the way but my job on this late afternoon was to get Nolizwi and her belongings from point A to point B. It had been a tiring day, the sun was setting, and I still hadn't eaten lunch. I didn't need or want another sick person to occupy my time. I knew what patients with this stage of AIDS needed and I knew it was well beyond my capacity on this particular day.

I started rationalizing to myself why this man actually didn't need my help. He had no connection to Itipini and I had never met him before. He was so sick that I could invest a tremendous amount of energy in him and he would likely still die shortly. Still, he was directly in front of me—almost literally under my nose—and it didn't seem right to pretend I had never seen him. The Gospel reading that Sunday in church had been about Jesus healing the paralytic who was lowered in from the roof by his friends. Tending to that person probably hadn't been on Jesus' list of things to do that day either.

I asked Granny about the man. "Oh, that one," she said. "He is very sick." It was a blinding statement of the obvious.

Reluctantly, I asked if he had been to a clinic and had any medical records around. Granny dug around in a bag under the bed and produced a tattered book. I flipped through it, hoping to learn that he was on the verge of being given antiretrovirals. He wasn't. They were still waiting for results of a CD4 count and only then would they be able to start the ARV process. But they were at least looking after him and had devised some means to get him to the clinic. He was "in the system" and that was all I would have been able to do for him anyway. Satisfied that my obligations were discharged—but not confident this man would live much longer—I handed the records back with some encouraging words about showing up for each appointment.

Nolizwi was finally ready and came out to say her goodbyes. Granny was effusive in her praise of me: "You have been blessed by Jesus with powers like his," she claimed. "You are helping Nolizwi a lot!" It was a kind thought but I laughed inside. My messianism was behind me. Seeing the sick man in bed had reminded me how helpless I usually felt. I wished Granny's perception matched reality.

Nolizwi was warmly welcomed by her new housemates, and in the following weeks she worked hard in school and our after-school group. She showed me her assignments from her classes and she was doing quite well, better than I ever could have hoped. Slowly, however, I started hearing little comments from her about the new living arrangements. They weren't complaints but they also weren't positive. "They say they don't have enough food for me." "We don't have any money for paraffin." "All we have is a little cornmeal." They were matter-of-fact comments, but the way she shyly chewed on her sleeve and avoided eye contact told me that it was a source of consternation for her and yet one more distraction.

Again, I was torn. I had hoped that once the housing had been arranged, I could return to my previous role of simply assuming that everyone had a place to return to after each class. But having been breached once, the barrier was hard to maintain. If I intervened in response to any of Nolizwi's comments, I would inject myself further into a situation from which I only wanted to withdraw. Yet I had come to know and like Nolizwi by this point and wanted so much to see her succeed in school. Our relationship made it impossible simply to ignore what amounted to pleas for help.

The balance I struck was unsatisfactory all around. On a handful of occasions, I gave Nolizwi a little money for food. But it was always insufficient and was not sustainable at all, given that it depended on my presence. Mostly, however, I told Nolizwi she needed to discuss the issues with the other people in the house. It wasn't easy to stare at a hungry person I considered my friend and tell her to look elsewhere for help. As she turned and walked away from me, I willed my mind to think about something else as quickly as possible.

Not long afterwards, I took a short break from Mthatha that coincided with the school's Easter break. It seemed as good a test of any as to how well Nolizwi could do without me around. It was nearly three weeks before I saw Nolizwi again. She was with the other students having a snack before an English session. We exchanged greetings and when I asked how she was, she said she was fine. My hopes rose that her living situation was improving. Then she handed me a letter, drafted in neat penmanship and surprisingly good English. I stepped away to read it.

Dear Jesse,

I'm no longer living in the place you gave me because of the behavior of the people I was living with. I thought I must live at Corana for a while just to relieve some stress they cause. Now I find it hard to go back there because of the way they make me feel. You cannot solve it because they are criticizing me and discriminating against me.

When you gave me food that I must go and prepare it for myself they ask me if it is going to cook itself or I will eat it raw because you give me no paraffin. I didn't bother by answering them but they kept on bullying me even wearing my clothes and my school clothes and even my blanket is their mat. Asiphe uses it as her baby's blanket when I am at school and I find it hard to use it at nights because of the smell of the baby's feces.

When I think about the situation they are putting me through they break my heart. I can have a place to live and my soul can rest because at Corana I am not bullied and they care about me and my education.

This situation is hard. You will also find it hard to solve it too but I hope that you will find a plan to solve it for me because I am desperate and I'm sure that I can not learn anything good while I still live with them.

The things that happen in these last months makes me think nothing good about my life. It's not my intentions to leave school because there's nobody at home who is educated and I want to be a good example but according to the situation I think I will drop out of school. And the fact of them abusing me is also adding to the stress of my mother lying in a bed useless and doing nothing for her children.

It ended with big letters scrawled across the bottom:

WHAT CAN I DO? PLEASE HELP ME.

There was a lot of activity in the Community Project area just then. A few women waited at the tap for water. A large group of children were clambering around the playground. Nolizwi was chatting with a few other students waiting for me to begin class. She still had a smile on her face and was laughing. How many other people in that scene had stories like Nolizwi's to tell? How many of those stories would I never know?

I had failed Nolizwi. I had made an effort to fix her problems for her and set her up in a situation that would allow her to focus on school. Instead, I had achieved exactly the opposite.

I called Nolizwi aside. I was proceeding blindly and didn't know what to say. I just didn't want to hurt her any further.

"Nolizwi," I said. "I'm sorry this has ended up this way."

She nodded.

"I want to make sure that you stay in school. It is very important that you keep studying hard."

"I know, Jesse. That's what I want to do."

"If you want to stay in Corana, I think that is the best plan." It was the only plan.

She nodded again.

I didn't know what else to say. Perhaps we could look for another living arrangement, but Nolizwi was right in her letter: in Corana, they had welcomed her in. She might as well return to a place where she was known.

The next day after school we drove to collect her final belongings she hadn't already moved on her own. Asiphe, the daughter, was there and was unfailingly polite to Nolizwi. While Nolizwi packed, I watched Asiphe cook a large pot of *umngqusho*, the traditional dish of corn and beans. If food had been a problem earlier, it wasn't on this day. My presence obviously changed the relationship between the two young women.

We drove the long road back to Corana and arrived again as the sun was setting. The rolling fields of the Transkei were as pretty as they had been on the last visit. In a very real way, we were right back where we started. I helped Nolizwi carry her things in. I wanted to see Granny again.

The emaciated man was gone and the bed he had been in had been moved. Granny didn't have a new wheelchair but she seemed in good spirits, cutting vegetables for a meal. There was a younger woman nearby helping her. I greeted them both. Granny responded with a bit of Xhosa too rapid for me to understand, though I caught the word for "food." I asked her to repeat herself.

The younger woman replied in English. "She wants to know if you can provide some money for food for Nolizwi."

"No, I'm sorry. We don't have any money for that."

Granny spoke again. I didn't understand.

"She says food is expensive."

"I know food is expensive but I don't have any money for that." I was getting frustrated. This was not the warm reception I had expected. Last time Granny had compared me to Jesus. Did she expect me to feed the five thousand this time?

"But Granny here is not even related to Nolizwi," the young woman said. "I am not related to Nolizwi. Granny just knows Nolizwi's mother from the village. And now her mother is sick. Her father . . ." She trailed off, waving her hand. Nolizwi was squirming quietly in a corner. I tried not to look at her. I imagined it was as uncomfortable for her as it was for me.

"That's very generous of her but I don't have any money for that."

It clearly was puzzling to the young woman that I wouldn't be able to support Nolizwi with an allowance for food. I explained about the Community Project and how Nolizwi came to the after-school program. I told her about how we helped families with school fees and money for uniforms and how I had tried to help Nolizwi find a place to live closer to school.

The young woman nodded. "You see, you and Granny need to work together to help Nolizwi."

"I agree," I said. "We paid her school fees and for her uniform and school supplies and help her after school. Maybe Granny can pay for the food."

The young woman laughed. "You must help her. You are her father now."

"No," I said firmly. "I am not. I am Nolizwi's friend." I stalked out. Nothing I had planned for Nolizwi was meeting my expectations.

I moved to South Africa full of good intentions and the desire to serve and even save people, to put their needs ahead of my own and figure out the ways in which I could help. It wasn't until I failed Nolizwi so dramatically that I realized the trouble with this way of thinking: it puts the onus of action—and responsibility—squarely on my shoulders. And the results of my actions, no matter how good my intentions, are beyond my control. That's doubly true when my actions were mediated through a series of cultural and language barriers I couldn't ever fully understand. I tried, and tried hard. And I failed. Nolizwi suffered and was hurt as a result of what I attempted to do.

As I drove away from Corana, I tried to be philosophical and focus not on the mistakes I made but on what I could learn from the experience. There was some comfort in the idea that the relationship Nolizwi and I had formed over the course of several months had intrinsic worth. I could see that value. I hoped Nolizwi did too. I would still be able to help Nolizwi after school for the remaining months I was in Itipini.

Nolizwi's story also forced me to acknowledge another truth. People in Itipini saw me as a problem solver. Nolizwi came to me when she was robbed because she thought I could fix her housing problem. Obviously, as I had just proven, these were spectacularly misplaced expectations. I barely knew what was going on most of the time. How could I be expected to solve problems the full contours of which I barely grasped? But each time someone approached me in that fashion, it further confirmed the idea that action was what was needed from me. And that, I realized on that drive away from Granny's house, is a sinful temptation. It put me at the center of the action. It made me the pivot point. It set me up as the actor who mattered most. It made me say to myself, "If they're looking to me for this, maybe I can do it." And I tried. And all I received was a letter from Nolizwi that I won't forget.

The better option, I realized, is to turn the situation around and ask, "Where is God? Where is grace at work?" But that takes time and energy and effort. It's easier to convince yourself you can snap your fingers and solve the problem yourself. And what would Nolizwi have done—recently robbed, in tears, and with no place to live—if I had said, "Where is God?" I don't know. I never let grace go to work.

Fifteen

"I Like Your Style"

I had become well established in Itipini. I taught English, collected re-payments from women, helped patients with AIDS, and navigated my way through the Xhosa environment with, if not ease, then at least func-tionality. My x-clicks, still weak, revealed I wasn't a native speaker, but I could make myself understood most of the time. The children were still eager to sing along with me, and they showed a certain degree of restraint in pummeling me with their attention. The staff members at the Community Project treated me as one of their own.

Makiwa, in particular, had welcomed me into her home. She worked faithfully in the kitchen day after day cooking for the preschool children and preparing a snack for the students after school. I occasion-ally gave her rides into town after work, and after several in succession she showed up at work one morning with a very large pumpkin from her garden as a sign of her thanks. I didn't want to take food she was growing for herself, but this was her response to my rides and it would have been ungrateful not to accept it. I ate pumpkin at every meal for the next sev-eral weeks. When I first arrived, Makiwa's youngest son, Simnikiwe, had been a shy two-year-old who clung to his mother all day in the kitchen. Now, he was a confident and outgoing four-year-old who happily took part in all the preschool activities. Simnikiwe's growth was one of the measures I used as a yardstick for my time in Itipini. He had come far. So had I.

Makiwa was married to Bafo, a security guard for an installation we passed on the drive to Itipini, and he and I smiled and waved to each other every day. Unlike many couples I knew in Itipini, Bafo and Makiwa doted on each other like young lovers. I often saw them walking hand in hand down the road.

It was a shock, then, to arrive one morning for work and learn that Bafo had died the previous night. He was overweight, and I knew he had diabetes, but his death still came as a surprise. The staff went over to Makiwa's home after work that afternoon, as we had when Thandeka died, and joined in prayer. Makiwa absented herself from work for a week or two to make arrangements and to mourn. I wondered how Simnikiwe was doing.

The funeral was in Bafo's rural village, an hour from Mthatha. I picked up several staff members in Itipini on a Saturday morning and they climbed into the back of the *bakkie*. I understood when they gave directions in Xhosa. When they started singing Xhosa choruses, I recognized them from our morning prayer circles and joined in.

It was a beautiful day in early summer and the rolling Transkei hills around Bafo's home were just beginning to shed their winter brown and turn green. There was a large tent set up for the occasion, and I could see groups of two and three people walking towards us on trails that wended their way through the various huts and buildings of the village. The crowd overflowed the tent and sat on the hills surrounding it listening to the priests and the family members eulogize Bafo. There was a time for other remembrances and the staff pushed me to stand up and say something. I spoke—in Xhosa—about how we would miss Bafo's smile and warmth on our drive to work each day.

After the service, we moved in procession to a nearby hill where a grave had been dug. Simnikiwe had been with Makiwa for much of the service but now he followed me to the burial. As his father was lowered into the ground, Simnikiwe held my hand, watching the proceedings intently. I wondered if he could comprehend that this was the last he would see of his father. The men began to shovel dirt and the women started singing a final song. Simnikiwe and I turned and hand in hand went back to the tent for the funeral meal.

If I needed any indication that I was a part of the Itipini community, this was it. I could sing and worship and speak with my colleagues, and they had seen it as natural and right that I should share that day with them and be their spokesperson. At a moment of grief, Simnikiwe turned to me for support. The uncertainty and distance I had felt in the first few months had vanished. I was completely enmeshed.

And yet it was coming time for me to leave. There were only a few months remaining in my second year and I had made plans to return to graduate school in the fall. On the quiet ride back to Mthatha from the funeral, I wondered how I could begin to disentangle myself. How would someone like Simnikiwe understand that I was leaving and wouldn't be back, at least not for a while?

⨏

These were the questions that weighed on my mind as I went about my routine in those final months in Itipini. Jenny returned to the United States for a while to see her family and raise more money, leaving Dorothy and me in charge of the clinic. I set up shop at Jenny's table and starting triaging patients for Dorothy.

We were a smoothly oiled machine, Dorothy and I, passing patients back and forth between us. In the course of a day, I found myself taking blood pressures, distributing TB pills, advising patients on how to begin the antiretroviral process, weighing and measuring babies, doing pregnancy and HIV tests, helping a hysterical woman with a bloody nose, giving a stern talking-to to another woman who had failed to retrieve her CD4 results from the Ngangalizwe health center for two months, and much more. The patients kept coming at us, fast and furiously, and we calmly and smoothly worked our way through each of them in turn. It was a wonder, I found myself thinking as I performed the fourth HIV test of the day, that I ever thought there wasn't enough for me to do in Itipini.

And that was just in the clinic. I found myself making more house calls, wandering down through the mud and past the pigs fighting over scraps, waving hello to the women making homebrew in front of their *shebeens*, dodging the mangy dogs that wandered in packs, and giving injections to patients who were so weak they could no longer walk. There I was, missionary to the core, dispensing medication in the midst of the trash and squalor of a shantytown, with pigs and dogs nosing nearby. To be so visibly helpful to so many people in Itipini made me feel competent in a way I never had before.

One morning, an older woman I knew well from her frequent trips to the clinic was carried in on the stretcher. She had been in a long decline and it was clear she was close to the end. I knelt down beside her and talked with her to learn what was wrong on this particular day. She was short of breath but was still able to grasp my hand tightly as she complained of a general weakness. To the other patients, I knew we were quite a scene. The tall, white, young American and the old, broken, and dying Xhosa woman together on the floor of the clinic. To me, however, in that moment, it felt natural and comfortable. I was speaking Xhosa and helping a woman I knew personally.

Dorothy knew this woman's story and watched our conversation as she treated other patients. As I gave the woman some pain medication and prepared to take her to the hospital, I heard Dorothy mutter under her breath, "Eh! I like your style." Could there be any greater affirmation, I wondered, than this from the woman who had once been so crusty and distant? She was my coworker now and I hers. We were a cross-cultural, multilingual treatment team. Who would have ever guessed it would be possible?

Outside of the clinic, my other concerns bumped along with reasonable success. My relations with the nurses at the Ngangalizwe health center were good, and Sister Nellie and I often found ourselves in wandering and discursive conversations that switched between Xhosa and English about patients, their health, and the health care system. I marveled at the change from how she once so intimidated me and how little I once knew about HIV and TB.

Ziyanda, one of the students who had made the most progress in English, showed me her report card after the first term and had an 80 percent in English, better even than she had done in Xhosa. Back home, I might have found it a middling grade, but in Mthatha 40 percent—no joke—counted as passing, and most of the students had trouble reaching even that. An 80 was beyond my wildest dreams. Ziyanda told me it was the second highest mark in the class. None of the other students did as well but most were passing.

Even Nolizwi wasn't doing too poorly. She continued to make the long walk to and from school each day, though now she supplemented her income by selling snacks during the midday break at school, which usually generated enough income for her to take a taxi in at least one direction. Her requests of me declined, either because she had fewer needs in Corana or because she knew I would say no. She did once ask for money to have new soles put on her shoes. Even with the taxi, her shoes were still doing a lot of walking. She also told me her ankle was hurting a lot. I wanted to tell her to stay off it for a while and give it a rest but that wasn't practical. She needed to get to and from school each day and her feet were the only way.

Pakama had more or less disappeared from my radar screen after that day I saw her walking in front of her shack. That was good. It meant she needed less attention and help. When I saw her now, it was remarkable to see how much weight she had gained. Far from the thin, weak figure I had once helped in and out of the car, she was now a plump woman with broad hips who walked around Itipini and into town with ease.

I learned something else about her one day, watching the women in an AIDS support group that Unathi had started work in their small garden. While most of the women were in the middle of the garden, digging and hoeing weeds to plant a new crop, Pakama had taken on more of a managerial role. She stood on the edge, pointing out where the weeds were, tsking when a woman missed one, and not letting any of the women leave their plot of land until it was absolutely clear. The other women seemed to take it in stride as part of Pakama's personality. Watching them work, I realized something new about Pakama. What I had once taken to be her strong will to live when she was so sick was really just her innate bossiness and desire to be in control expressing itself in a different way. Whatever. It had been the difference between life and death for her.

Petros was still in prison and I continued to make sporadic visits. He said he lost *The BFG* and the paper I had given him when he had been transferred to a different section. He didn't ask for soap or anything else, which was a relief. But that didn't leave us much else to talk about. He told me about the ongoing delays in his court case. About the only thing I could think to tell him was how his sister's son was learning to walk. The conversations lasted ten minutes or so before I started making noises about all the work to do back at the clinic. I hoped the fact of my visit alone was enough of a signal to Petros that he wasn't forgotten but it was still difficult. We had never had much of a relationship to begin with and there was almost nothing to build on in prison.

Yoliswa, whose business of selling clothes had collapsed and caused such great despair, weighed heaviest on my mind. I imagined her in some run-down hovel with an abusive boyfriend who didn't care for her or her children. It wasn't a pretty picture, but I didn't know what to do and I still shrank from confronting such an obvious failure. Finally—six months too late—I summoned my courage and called the last number I had for Yoliswa. She picked up on the second ring and I told her who it was. I was tentative, not sure how she would respond.

But she was her cheery self and greeted me warmly.

"Where are you living now?" I asked.

She named a village not far from Mthatha. "You should come see me," she said in the tone of voice I knew so well from the days when I saw her cheery and bubbly around Itipini, returning the Disney picture books to the library.

So one Saturday I got in the car and followed her directions out of town. When I pulled off the main road, I called Yoliswa and told her I had arrived. Not fifteen seconds later, Bongamusa, her young son, came tearing around the corner of the nearest building, screaming in delight, and crashed into my knees. I lifted him up and he smiled broadly to see me again.

Yoliswa came walking around the corner and she looked the same as ever. No black eyes, no bruises, no significant weight loss. She was still an asymptomatic HIV patient. We hugged and she showed me her new home. It was a good-sized home in a quiet corner of the village. Yoliswa explained that it belonged to family friends and she was looking after it while they worked in Johannesburg. In the meantime, she was attending the small church that had been started by another family friend in the village. She taught Sunday school, made sure her children attended, and lived off the grants she received for them. Without prompting she brought up the question of the loan.

"I'm sorry I didn't pay you back," she said. "After my aunt asked me to leave, I needed the money for food and clothes for the children."

It was as I feared, and I just nodded.

"It was a good business," she said wistfully, and there was a hint of a question in her voice, as if maybe I wanted to help her start again. But it was too late to launch anything new. I demurred and asked instead about her health. She was overdue for a CD4 count and I encouraged her to visit the Itipini clinic. In those remaining weeks and months, I saw her occasionally, either in Itipini or at her new home. Our grand plans to lift Yoliswa out of poverty had come to naught and—other than her new, temporary home—she was in no different position than when I had first met her. It was a familiar story by this point for me.

In my early days in Itipini, when I struggled with not *doing* anything, I took comfort from the fact that my presence was important and that who I could *be* was significant. Ironically, now that I had reached a point where I was *doing* plenty, my *being* was suffering. My patience, never very great to begin with, stretched to the point of breaking. My temper was too short. I snapped at patients who cut in line. I let frustrating days in the clinic affect my mood during the English classes. I began to view everything I encountered through cynical lenses. People asking for money weren't just poor, they were trying to scam me. Sometimes, I was unpleasant to be around.

The trouble was that I was just too much in demand and—my experience with Nolizwi or Yoliswa conveniently set aside—I was convinced I could help people who asked, if not in large ways at least in small ones. But too many people were looking to me to solve their problems—small and large—and I couldn't bear the burden. I became suspicious of each request for assistance. I didn't believe mothers when they said their children needed help buying shoes for school. Despite my best efforts with the microcredit program, I still found myself dealing with money. When Mkuseli and I went shopping, it became almost physically painful to purchase items for school. Once, while walking back to the car with a load of purchases for the students, I almost broke down in tears. My stomach hurt and I struggled to carry the bags. I knew the students needed uniforms to be admitted to school, but I simply no longer believed in buying the uniforms for them. Giving money and giving things wasn't successful or sustainable. I did want to help remove obstacles to their education, but each time I bought something for someone, I could only think about how it was encouraging them to see me as their personal bank and problem solver. Buying stuff wasn't sharing an existence and it wasn't building relationships. In fact, it corroded relationships.

I began to start saying no to people. A college student who lived near Itipini sought help from me for her tuition fees. I knew of a scholarship she could apply for and directed her towards that, but she kept coming back, looking for help with her assignments. I helped as I could but I wasn't ready to begin a new relationship with someone so soon before my departure. One day as she was leaving, she said, "When I have trouble in school, I will come to you for help." I nodded, conceal- ing my reluctance. Then there came the inevitable request, phrased as a statement. "I do not have the money for the taxi to get home." I told her that she would have to walk and that if she wanted to come back for help in the future she would have to pay her own way. Her mouth set. "That means you don't care about me," she said. I shrugged, but internally I was seething. I wanted her to do well—I wanted everyone to do well—but I hated the sense of expectation she was placing on me.

The attitude carried over to my work in the clinic as well. For some patients, I was tender and close and caring. But for others, I could barely find the energy to care. Xolisa was an HIV-positive tuberculosis patient who had defaulted on his treatment six months after I arrived and then disappeared. I looked around for him at the time but no one seemed to know much about him. He was carried back into the clinic on the stretcher after nearly a year's absence, almost literally in his death throes. His eyes were sunk deep in his face and he could barely move his emaci- ated arms and legs. I looked him over but it was clear there wasn't much we could do in the clinic. He needed to be in the hospital so I directed the friends who carried him in to load him into the *bakkie* and we drove off. The hospital was the same scene I knew from so many previous trips, beginning with Fumanekile—overwhelmingly busy, with patients in the hallways, a long line waiting to be seen, and no one obviously in charge. I distractedly showed his friends where to wait and headed back to the clinic. Later that afternoon, to no one's surprise, we learned Xolisa had died at the hospital.

I couldn't help comparing my reaction to Xolisa to what had hap- pened when Fumanekile died. The situations were the same. Both had been quite sick with similar conditions. But whereas with Fumanekile I had been active and engaged, cutting in line to ensure that he was seen, I could barely be bothered with Xolisa. I hadn't even helped lift the stretcher. But what could I have done? Xolisa should have completed his TB treatment a year earlier. That—along with regular CD4 counts— would almost certainly have prevented him from reaching the point where he was lying, practically dead, on the clinic floor. I knew by now that there were reasons people defaulted on their treatment, but it was still hard to do more than shrug and move on to the next patient. I had more experience. I didn't care less overall, but I could see situations in which it made less sense to invest my time and energy.

A friend wrote me around this time and said it sounded like I was getting burned out on Itipini. I recoiled from the phrase and immediately wrote a defensive reply. Of course I wasn't burned out. Wasn't I now more effective than I had ever been before? Weren't more people turning to me for help? Wasn't I speaking Xhosa with ease, dispensing medication, ordering food, paying staff, buying clothes, teaching English, collecting repayments from borrowers, and generally keeping everything functioning? There were new Pakamas and Sizekas all the time and—Xolisa aside—I was working with many of them in just the same way I had worked with the first AIDS patients I had encountered. How could I be burned out?

I knew I wasn't burned out on Africa or the poor or mission or service. But perhaps, I acknowledged, I was reaching my limit in Itipini. I had come to fill the role of problem solver of too many simultaneous problems. That role, I realized, was unsustainable. I started looking for ways out. I started looking for ways to disengage and reduce my involvement with the community.

In search of a good way to do this, I started pawing through our medical records. The years of use had resulted in some that had been lost in the shuffle, misfiled, or otherwise misplaced. I began to methodically go through each drawer, removing patients who no longer lived in Itipini, re-alphabetizing, and generally straightening up the files. When I had arrived in Itipini, I had done almost exactly the same thing as I looked through cards in that frustrating search each time a new patient walked in. I had yearned at the time for something more constructive and meaningful to do. Now, I was back with the cards. Only this time I turned to the cards to get away from all the constructive and meaningful tasks I had found—and failed—to do. The cards had become my refuge.

I had come to completely inhabit the missionary role. I identified myself as "a missionary of the Episcopal Church" to anyone who asked, in stark contrast to the reluctance with which I took on the title two years earlier.

My final weeks in Itipini gave me a chance to think back again to what it meant to be a missionary.

The experience with people like Nolizwi had confirmed for me something I had read and learned at training but never entirely understood: mission belongs to God, not us. God's mission has, from the beginning of the Bible, been the same—the restoration of right relationship among people and between people and God. This is the mission of reconciliation; to use a Hebrew word, it is about building up *shalom*, the completeness and wholeness we find only in God. Received, forgiven, and transformed by God in baptism, it becomes our ongoing role to figure out what part of that mission we are called to share in.

The metaphor of journey is one of the oldest descriptions of religious faith—for good reason, too, as there are many journeys in the Bible. Abraham set out to a land he did not know, Moses and the Israelites wandered into the desert, Jonah took off in the wrong direction, Naomi returned home after years away, Paul sailed around the Mediterranean. Journey is an apt metaphor for mission as well. The missionary's role is to share a journey with others. When that journey travels a path the missionary knows well, he can show others the way. When that journey ventures into unfamiliar territory, the missionary lets others lead. Leadership on this journey is one of many things that is both given and received. When the territory is unknown to everyone, everyone moves forward together—in faith—confident in the knowledge that they are not alone. And always the missionary is pushing, prodding, and poking the journey in the direction of *shalom*.

The ministry of Jesus himself was a journey. In the Gospels, it is remarkable how often Jesus himself is said to have left a place, arrived someplace else, crossed the sea, or headed towards Jerusalem. Jesus' ministry was not a stationary one. Neither should ours be. But Jesus also journeyed, in a sense, from heaven to earth and in the Incarnation crossed a hitherto impassable barrier. It is this fundamental decision to share an existence with humanity that precedes Jesus' journey to the reconciling moments of the cross and empty tomb.

My experience of being incarnate in Itipini had two important impacts. The first is that it allowed me to make real—or reify—the experience of life in Itipini in a way that simply reading about it from afar could not. In watching people die from HIV, suffer in a broken home, or search for income, I learned much about the obstacles that impair their relationship with the world around them. This is where mission begins: the decision to show up and share an existence with people who may not seem much like us but are equally children of God and equally yearn for right relationship with the world around them. My incarnational decision was to get on a plane to Mthatha and step out of the *bakkie* on that first day. From that flowed everything else.

As their life experience was made real for me, I began to build relationships with people in Itipini. If they hadn't seen me as a credible partner, or I couldn't have communicated with them, then our mutual journey towards reconciliation would have gone nowhere. Jesus did the same thing, forming close relationships with a core group of people who spread his reconciling message far and wide. If I did anything that moved anyone towards reconciliation, it started with forming deep relationships with people—Pakama, Nolizwi, Fumanekile, and so many more. This is why emphasizing *being* over *doing* in mission is so important. We draw closer to one another more because of who we *are* around each other, and less because of what we *do* for each other.

As in school, there are three Rs in mission: reify, relate, reconcile.

There are obstacles along the way, of course, speed bumps and roadblocks along the journey. A major one for me in Itipini was the language barrier, which still was present even after I gained functionality in Xhosa. Another obstacle was the culture barriers. These manifested themselves in countless circumstances, like when Lindumzi cited myths and falsehoods about antiretroviral medications as justification for not taking them. Other obstacles are internally imposed and shared by all. When I got angry at the preschool children or snapped at a patient, I was revealing the same sinfulness that impedes God's mission all over the world. This same sin is manifest in the unfairness of the world we have created. People may find their journey stymied by a lack of jobs, sickness and death from preventable illnesses, and much more.

But the major obstacle I ran into again and again had to do with the people of Itipini themselves. Desmond Tutu once wrote, "True reconciliation is a deeply personal mater. It can happen only between persons who assert their own personhood and who acknowledge and respect that of others." It was relatively easy for me to assert my own personhood because I had been raised to think that way. (Asserting it graciously was another matter, mind you.) In Itipini, I realized people had trouble expressing who God created them to be. Many of them had spent a lifetime watching people who seemed to be more talented become a lot more successful. They saw these people in town, on the news, and in the dominant cultural messages. Perhaps they'd tried to work their way out of their difficult circumstances and failed, or perhaps the idea of actually changing their lives seemed so ludicrous they didn't even want to try. Whatever the reason, on some level there is a psychological barrier at work, like when Sizeka waited so long to begin trying for ARVs. But at the very core, every person is a unique child of God blessed with certain gifts. This is not insignificant. The challenge is getting people to look away from what surrounds them and look instead to the magnitude of the gift that lies within. This is not easy, especially when those same people may have already given up hope, allowing their talents to lie fallow deep within them. To return to the metaphor of a journey, they either don't realize they are on a journey or don't realize when it is their turn to lead. Instead, they keep turning to people like me to show them the way, even though they know it better than me.

The key mission task then is not helping people start businesses or getting people the right medications. The first mission task is to draw out the inherent talent and dignity of each person we encounter so they can journey onwards and draw others along with them. They must realize the capacity and wonder that lies within them and how that can change their lives. In so doing, we will no doubt find they draw talents out of us that we were not aware of. How do we get people in Itipini—and everywhere—to realize that it is in their power to set out on a new journey, one pointed towards *shalom*?

Although I identified as a missionary, others who observed my work from afar may not have seen much difference between me and the average Peace Corps volunteer. My motivations weren't all that different: I wanted to see a new part of the world and help people as I could. I didn't baptize anyone. I didn't use the Bible any more than anyone else. Indeed, I replaced the after-school Bible study with *Charlie and the Chocolate Factory*. I didn't preach or teach religious education, as missionary friends of mine in Mthatha did. But to say this is not to say that Christ was never present in Mthatha or in my work. Indeed, it is the model and method of Christ's life—especially his Incarnation—that shaped my approach to the work. I was most aware of the transforming power of Christ on me.

Moreover, many people in Itipini were already as deeply Christian as me. They didn't need to be converted. But what they did need was the knowledge that God cares not only for their future salvation but their present health and welfare. The poverty in Itipini was a result of dysfunctional and impaired relationships. Restoring those relationships was the key missional task. What makes this work different to secular development work is the mindset that missionaries bring to it. In order to build up people and truly "empower" them, we must do so with reference to a Creator God, who lovingly created each person with a divine purpose and gifted them to fulfill that purpose. Religious education, then, seems to be a necessary part of truly sustainable—and ostensibly secular—development. Christian missionaries bring to development and the work of poverty relief a whole panoply of tools that secular agencies do not.

Mission, I realized, is foundational to faith. It is our response to God's outpouring of love to us, and it is the way we work towards the kingdom of God that, we believe, is both here now and will come again when Christ returns. I was hopelessly misguided to think that I could save the people of Itipini. Christ has already saved the world. My job— and the job of all Christians—is to discern my share of the mission of reconciliation and prepare for Christ's return. But many of my supporters wrote to me to say my experience in Itipini could seem distant and extreme, working on a garbage dump in a foreign land. This only reinforces the misperception that mission is something only for people who want to move across the world for a few years. The entire world is crying out for right relationships. There are places in each community in every country in desperate need of *shalom*.

But we shouldn't think mission is easy. Sometimes the very places in the world that are most in need of *shalom* are the places we are told to stay away from because they are unsafe or the people are so different from us. It's hard to be incarnate when everyone is telling us to go someplace, anyplace else. It's worth remembering, then, that Jesus' decision to be incarnate ended in his crucifixion. Incarnational mission demands sacrifice, not a popular concept in a world that is more and more focused on creating needs that don't exist and in a church that wants to do nothing that might scare people away. What we sacrifice in mission is our security, the barriers we consciously and unconsciously erect to keep us safe. Mission, then, requires vulnerability. It's not the forced vulnerability of an abused spouse or neglected child but the chosen vulnerability of one who is confident of God's loving protection and confident of his role in God's plan for the world.

As I prepared to leave Itipini and return to the United States to begin my journey in a new place, the question I faced is the same all Christians face everywhere: how do I take my place in God's mission in the place where I am? How can I be incarnate in a new "place" even if that place is the same community I've spent my entire life in? How can I build relationships with people who are different from me? How can I share a journey with someone else and nudge it in the direction of *shalom*?

The obstacles to *shalom* are not insignificant. This rosy picture of the journey of mission can seem false and distant compared to the reality of a life like Fumanekile's or Lindumzi's. We want so much to be able to snap our fingers and solve the problems of the world. Ultimately what matters, I realized, is not where the journey ends up—none of us will ever live to see the perfect peace of the kingdom of God on earth—but that we choose to set out on the journey at all. The journey of mission is its destination.

I picked a Friday in early May to formally announce my departure, six weeks before my last plane flight out of Mthatha. In the clinic that morning before prayers, I sat down with Dorothy and Mkuseli and told them the news. Mkuseli looked like the wind had been knocked out of him. Dorothy gave the quick shake of her head and sharp intake of breath she usually gave when someone died. I quickly stressed that the Episcopal Church was sending a replacement. "He won't be like you," Dorothy said and looked away. Hoping I could cheer them up by pinning the blame for my departure on God, I said I was returning to school to study theology. Even that didn't help. "We need you here," Mkuseli said.

The rest of the staff and community members took the news somewhat better, in a spirit of resignation. All white people left at some point. They knew I wasn't from Mthatha. It had only been a matter of time.

I began to make my rounds of other friends. Vuyelwa, who had finally had an HIV test after so many months of conversation, was now working at a hair salon in town. I occasionally visited her there and on this day asked her to step outside. When I told her I was leaving, she stamped her foot on the sidewalk. "Jesse, this is very bad news!" she said firmly and stomped back into the salon.

I told Yoliswa as well, and she sighed, but I had played such a small role in her life in the last few months that I wouldn't be missed much. Bongamusa took it much harder. He crossed his three-year-old arms and glowered at me. I tried to cheer him up by smiling but he only looked away and glowered harder. After a few minutes I gave up and went to leave. Yoliswa waved as I drove away and encouraged Bongamusa to do the same but he didn't change. His sullen gaze stared at me through the rearview mirror.

It was the preschool children I was most worried about. I could communicate with them as well as with any adults, but I wasn't sure they would understand that when I said I was "going away," I meant for good. My early efforts weren't too successful. When I said I was leaving to go to school, one young girl took my hand and pointed up the hill. "You can study at Ezra school with us!" When I explained I needed to go to a special school to study theology, another student asked if she could come with me. "It's a long way," I said.

"That's okay," she said, pointing to the *bakkie*. "I'll just ride in the back." How could I explain about planes and long flights and the ocean that lay between us and divinity school? Given the number of children who had at one point or another called me Jesus, I thought I should just say, "Where I am going, you cannot come." Eventually, the message got through, but in a particularly Transkeian way. According to the children, I was going to the rural areas, not an uncommon move for people in Itipini and something that well accorded with their sense of the world. Satisfied they knew that I wouldn't be back, I let the matter lie.

Jenny returned from her fundraising tour and I turned things over to her, content with alphabetizing cards, finishing off *The BFG* with the English class, leaving the microcredit program in position for a successor to step in, and reprising our greatest hits with the preschool children. On the final morning I stopped to explain that this was the last time I would play the guitar with them. I knew the message got through because tears started to leak from the eyes of a few students. Our last dance through "Johnny B. Goode" was with tearstained cheeks, my own as much as anyone else's.

I found myself thinking back to that first windy evening in East London two years earlier when I had dinner with Lebo at the drive-through restaurant while we waited for our bus. Right after she told me that I had ruined my life by moving to South Africa, she paused and thought again. "But for you," she said, "it might not be so bad. You can leave whenever you want."

That was true. I had had my "experience" of Africa and was now choosing to leave, something that none of my new friends in Itipini could do as easily. It was part of the privilege of my birth and upbringing that I could parachute in for two years—an infinitesimal amount of time by anyone's standards except those of a twenty-something-year-old—immerse myself in the community, and then walk out.

But Lebo had been wrong. I hadn't ruined my life. No, my life had been transformed, my journey redirected, by glimpses of God's grace in this particular community of God's children. The paths of our journeys were diverging, true. But the memories I took with me continue to shape the trajectory of mine.

Author's Note

In Chinua Achebe's *Things Fall Apart*, the District Commissioner considers the suicide of Okonkwo, the protagonist, and thinks, "The story of this man who had killed a messenger and hanged himself would make interesting reading. One could almost write a whole chapter on him. Perhaps not a whole chapter but a reasonable paragraph, at any rate." The irony, of course, is that the comments come at the end of an entire book about Okonkwo's life.

I fear I have been guilty of the District Commissioner's sin, reducing people in Itipini to paragraphs and chapters when each one of them—and many others—deserves an entire book. I ask their forgiveness and remind the reader of the complexities of every human life that cannot be fully expressed in written words. My inadequacies as a writer are poor repayment for the way the people of Itipini opened their lives to me and made me a part of their community during my time there. So many of them—including those who feature in this book and those who do not—are deeply imprinted on my being. To name them all would take another book.

In the course of writing, I have changed some names and altered some chronological details to preserve anonymity and maintain narrative flow. Sizeka is a composite character. Most of the chapters were first drafted while I still lived in Mthatha, soon after events took place. The dialogue is based on my recollections and journal and blog entries. That blog, featuring more stories of people in Itipini, will remain online indefinitely—http://mthathamission.blogspot.com.

My understanding of the position of Xhosa men in chapter 13 comes primarily from Jonny Steinberg's *Sizwe's Test* (published as *Three Letter Plague* in South Africa), a terrific look at the effect of AIDS in one

Transkeian village. Steinberg's books are required reading for all who want to understand post-apartheid South Africa. My understanding of HIV/AIDS was shaped significantly by the contrasting perspectives in Helen Epstein's *The Invisible Cure* and Eileen Stillwaggon's *AIDS and the Ecology of Poverty*. Nelson Mandela's *Long Walk to Freedom* and the books of Mark Gevisser, Edwin Cameron, Zakes Mda, and Allister Sparks have all helped me come to grips with South Africa.

Numerous people have supported me during the writing of this book and to them I express my thanks. Mary Brennan planted the idea for a book, and countless readers of my blog posts and e-mail newsletters encouraged it. Sarah Jackson, David Ross, Andrew Hankinson, Rachel Watson, Eric Tipler, Ann Phelps, Stephen Register, Nathan Suhr-Sytsma, Ashley Makar, and Ashley Hurst all provided important feedback on individual chapters, helping me sharpen and hone the text. Jared Duval and Paul-Gordon Chandler had helpful advice on navigating the publishing process.

Living in a foreign culture is often an isolating and lonely experience. Joe and Anna Sawatzky were dear friends and colleagues in Mthatha who went a long way to ameliorating those feelings. Errol and Audrey Theophilius, Pat and Zama Gabeda, Florence Chikwebani, Xoliswa Mxakaza, Lwazikazi Madikiza, and Piwe Kobo were good friends as well. Matthew Kellen, Sarah Jackson, Stephen Mazingo, Cortney Dale, Robin Denney, and John Simpson were great friends and fellow missionaries. The brothers at Mariya uMama weThemba Monastery were wonderfully supportive and provided a place where some of these chapters were first drafted. Most of all, Jenny McConnachie and her late husband Chris were the kind of missionaries I can only ever aspire to be. The way they welcomed a clueless but energetic young missionary in their lives speaks volumes about their Christian virtue.

I'm blessed with parents who support their sons even when they hare off to random corners of the globe. None of this would have been possible without the absolute support and encouragement of my parents, Tom and Beth.